CORE ADVA

MW00889873

Unit 9

Making Sense of
Exponents

DR. RANDY PALISOC

IRONBOX®
Education

IRONBOX®
Education

Printed in the United States.

Contents

Essential Background Information

Making Sense of Exponents

About the Author

My name is Dr. Randy Palisoc, and I'm on a mission to give kids **Power Over Numbers** and **Power Over Learning.**

I am a former classroom teacher, and I was a founder of the **five-time national award winning** Synergy Academies, whose elementary school was named the **#1 Urban Elementary School in America** by the National Center for Urban School Transformation in 2013.

The reason I designed this system is that too many students do not have a strong foundation in math, and they do not "get" the standard explanations found in many textbooks. This is troubling because students who struggle early on are often unable catch up to their peers later in life.

On the other hand, students who do have strong foundations have a greater shot at success later in life. In 2013, for example, students who were with Synergy since elementary school (all minority students) had a 95% pass rate on the California High School Exit Exam, compared to only about 79% statewide (all ethnicities).

As shown above, **strong foundations really do matter.**

The Core Advantage math fluency system by Ironbox Education is designed to build those foundations and to build fluency as quickly and as easily as possible. It does so by thinking like kids and teaching in a way that makes sense to them.

I designed this math fluency system based on my experience working with thousands of students from elementary school through high school and finding out what makes them successful. I hope you are able to use this system to give your students or children Power Over Numbers™ and Power Over Learning™!

Dr. Randy Palisoc received his Bachelor of Science degree from the University of Southern California (USC), his Master of Education degree from the University of California, Los Angeles (UCLA), and his Doctor of Education degree from USC.

Making Sense of Exponents

An Exponential Effect on Learning

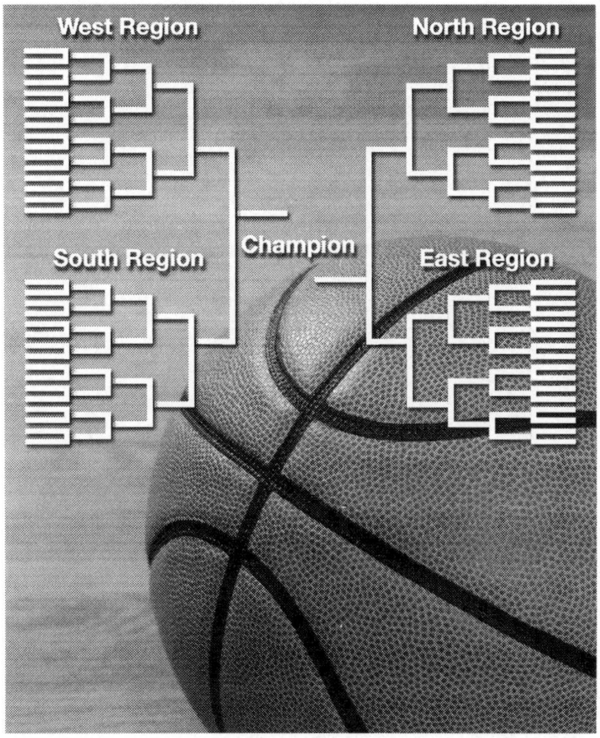

An exponent is a simple idea that captures the powerful concept of repeated multiplication. Exponents find their way into many real-life situations. Here are two examples:

- $2^6 = 2 \times 2 \times 2 \times 2 \times 2 \times 2 = 64$
  The number of teams to invite to a six-round single-elimination tournament
- $\$100{,}000(1.08)^{10} = \$215{,}892.50$
  The amount that $100,000 will grow to by earning 8% interest per year, compounded annually for 10 years

With repeated multiplication, numbers can become very big very quickly. In other words, they grow exponentially.

Additionally, when students are fluent working with exponents, it has an exponential effect on learning. It helps them crack the code to higher level math concepts such as factoring quadratic expressions and using scientific notation.

Making Sense of Exponents builds fluency by helping students notice the nuances involved with working with exponents.

How does this system work?

First things first.

Since exponents involve working with repeated multiplication, students must be fluent with their multiplication facts. Students will add, subtract, multiply, and divide numbers and variables with exponents. The exponents will include positive integers and negative integers, which will result in fractions. As you can see, this unit involves many prerequisite skills. Therefore, please make sure students have gone through the following units first as they contain the most important prerequisite skills for this unit:

- *10 Powerful Steps to Multiplication Fluency*
- *Making Sense of Division*
- *Making Sense of Fractions*
- *Making Sense of Integers*

The Core Advantage series is different from ordinary workbooks. The system is designed to have students work interactively on short, easy-to-understand guided lessons with their teacher or their parent. The reason for this is that when students (especially young students) work with an actual person, it makes learning a much more personal and meaningful experience. ***The human touch matters.***

It's important for teachers or parents to watch the lesson-by-lesson demo videos. This way, they'll know the key nuances to point out, and it takes the guesswork and confusion out of the lesson. There are also fully-annotated answer keys that not only show the answer, but also show the steps involved in getting there.

Each lesson provides students with well-thought-out, purposeful practice to promote fluency, and all the lessons build systematically upon each other. The following page provides a suggested pacing plan, and you can adjust the pacing as needed.

Pacing: Making Sense of Exponents

Making Sense of Exponents involves many prerequisite skills, including multiplication, division, fractions, and integers. *Therefore, please make sure students have gone through the following units first as they contain the most important prerequisite skills for this unit:*

- *10 Powerful Steps to Multiplication Fluency*
- *Making Sense of Division*
- *Making Sense of Fractions*
- *Making Sense of Integers*

A sample pacing plan for this unit is shown below, and the pacing can be adjusted as necessary.

	Monday	Tuesday	Wednesday	Thursday	Friday
Week 1	Lesson 1 Using Exponents to Show Repeated Multiplication Lesson 2 Graphing Repeated Addition vs. Repeated Multiplication	Lesson 3 Exponents (1, 10, Fractions, and Integers as Bases) Lesson 4 Exponential Growth	Lesson 5 Single-Elimination Tournament Lesson 6 The National Championship Tournament	Lesson 7 Adding and Subtracting Variables with Exponents	Lesson 8 Adding and Subtracting Variables with Exponents Lesson 9 Multiplying Binomials
Week 2	Lesson 10 Multiplying Binomials Lesson 11 Multiplying Variables with Exponents	Lesson 12 Dividing Variables with Exponents Lesson 13 Dividing Variables with Exponents (Negative Exponents)	Lesson 14 Multiplying Variables with Exponents (Negative Exponents) Lesson 15 Multiplying and Dividing Variables with Exponents	Lesson 16 Multiplying and Dividing Variables with Exponents Lesson 17 Comparing Numbers with Exponents	Lesson 18 Scientific Notation
Week 3	Lesson 19 Scientific Notation Lesson 20 Exponents Review	Lesson 21 Exponents Review Lesson 22 Diamond Puzzles	Lesson 23 Factoring Quadratic Expressions Lesson 24 Diamond Puzzles	Lesson 25 Factoring Quadratic Expressions	Lesson 26 Factoring Quadratic Expressions to Simplify Fractions
Week 4	Lesson 27 Using the Distributive Property to Multiply Polynomials Lesson 28 Multiplying Binomials Using the FOIL Method	Lesson 29 Multiplying Binomials Using the FOIL Method (or the FIOL Method)	Lesson 30 Multiplying Binomials Using the FOIL Method (or the FIOL Method)	Lesson 31 Multiplying Binomials Using the FOIL Method (or the FIOL Method) Lesson 32 Adding and Subtracting Numbers with Exponents	Lesson 33 Adding, Subtracting, and Multiplying Numbers with Exponents
Week 5	Lesson 34 Comparing Numbers with Exponents	Lesson 35 Comparing Numbers with Exponents	Lesson 36 Comparing Fractions with Exponents		

Addressing State Learning Standards or the Common Core State Standards

Today, schools across America are either using their own state's learning standards or the Common Core State Standards.

No matter what learning standards a school is using, this system helps give students an academic advantage by building fluency faster than has been possible in the past. Fluency is important for all students because it helps them be more precise, which in turn helps them more easily make sense of math.

Take a look at these two Standards for Mathematical Practice (MP), which are used by states using the Common Core State Standards:

> MP #1: Make sense of problems and persevere in solving them.
> MP #6: Attend to precision.

How do these two math practices go together?

- If students ***cannot*** attend to precision (#6), then they will not make sense of problems (#1), and they will not persevere in solving them (#1).

On the other hand,

- If students ***can*** attend to precision (#6), then they are more likely to make sense of problems (#1) and are more likely to persevere in solving them (#1).

As you can see, attending to precision (#6) can mean the difference between confidence and confusion.

The unique Core Advantage system used in this book can help give students an academic advantage in a short amount of time. It is designed to build fluency so that students can attend to precision (#6) and actually understand what they're doing in math.

It does take hard work and practice on the part of students, and only students themselves can determine their level of success based on their effort. The good news is that the greater their level of fluency, the more confidence students will have, and the more likely they are to persevere and put in that necessary hard work and practice.

Fluency matters, and I hope that you are able to use this system to build that fluency with your students.

-- Dr. Randy Palisoc

Name______________________________

Making Sense of

Exponents

Part 1 – The Foundation

Go down your **Success Tracker** in the order shown below, and write your score for each of the activities as you complete them. The goal is to make any corrections necessary to earn a score of 100%.

	Lesson	Lesson Name	Score
KEY LESSON	1	Using Exponents to Show **Repeated Multiplication**	
KEY LESSON	2	**Graphing** Repeated Addition vs. Repeated Multiplication	
KEY LESSON	3	Exponents (1, 10, Fractions, and Integers as Bases)	
KEY LESSON	4	**Exponential Growth**	
KEY LESSON	5	Single-Elimination Tournament	
	6	The National Championship Tournament	
KEY LESSON	7	**Adding and Subtracting Variables with Exponents**	
	8	Adding and Subtracting Variables with Exponents	
KEY LESSON	9	**Multiplying Binomials**	
	10	Multiplying Binomials	
KEY LESSON	11	**Multiplying Variables with Exponents**	
KEY LESSON	12	**Dividing Variables with Exponents**	
KEY LESSON	13	Dividing Variables with Exponents **(Negative Exponents)**	
KEY LESSON	14	Multiplying Variables with Exponents (Negative Exponents)	
	15	Multiplying and Dividing Variables with Exponents	
	16	Multiplying and Dividing Variables with Exponents	
KEY LESSON	17	**Comparing Numbers with Exponents**	

Making Sense of

Exponents

Part 2 – Applications

Go down your **Success Tracker** in the order shown below, and write your score for each of the activities as you complete them. The goal is to make any corrections necessary to earn a score of 100%.

	Lesson	Lesson Name	Score
KEY LESSON	18	**Scientific Notation**	
	19	Scientific Notation	
	20	Exponents Review	
	21	Exponents Review	
KEY LESSON	22	Diamond Puzzles	
KEY LESSON	23	**Factoring Quadratic Expressions**	
	24	Diamond Puzzles	
	25	Factoring Quadratic Expressions	
KEY LESSON	26	Factoring Quadratic Expressions to Simplify Fractions	
KEY LESSON	27	**Using the Distributive Property to Multiply Polynomials**	
KEY LESSON	28	**Multiplying Binomials Using the FOIL Method**	
KEY LESSON	29	Multiplying Binomials Using the FOIL Method (or the FIOL Method)	
KEY LESSON	30	Multiplying Binomials Using the FOIL Method (or the FIOL Method)	
	31	Multiplying Binomials Using the FOIL Method (or the FIOL Method)	
KEY LESSON	32	**Adding and Subtracting Numbers with Exponents**	
KEY LESSON	33	**Adding, Subtracting, and Multiplying Numbers with Exponents**	
KEY LESSON	34	**Comparing Numbers with Exponents**	
	35	Comparing Numbers with Exponents	
KEY LESSON	36	**Comparing Fractions with Exponents**	

KEY LESSON

Name______________________________________

Lesson 1: Using Exponents to Show Repeated Multiplication

Use an exponent as a shortcut for writing ***repeated multiplication.***

Example: $2 \times 2 \times 2 \times 2 = 2^4$ base → 2^4 ← exponent "2 to the 4th power"

Part 1: Expand first, then evaluate.

Example: $2^4 = 2 \cdot 2 \cdot 2 \cdot 2$ $= 16$	A. 2^3	B. 2^5
C. 7^2	D. 8^2	E. 9^2
F. 5^3	G. 3^4	H. 4^4
I. 10^2	J. 10^3	K. 10^6

Part 2: Expand to show repeated multiplication.

L. m^3	M. s^2	N. y^5

Part 3: Simplify using exponents.

O. $12 \times 12 \times 12 \times 12 \times 12$	P. $n \cdot n \cdot n \cdot n \cdot n \cdot n \cdot n$	Q. $x \cdot x \cdot x \cdot x \cdot y \cdot y \cdot y \cdot y \cdot y \cdot z \cdot z$
R. $(n)(n)(n)(n)$	S. $(x+1)(x+1)(x+1)(x+1)$	T. $7(x-3)(x-3)(x-3)(m+5)$

Name_____________________________

Lesson 2: Graphing Repeated Addition vs. Repeated Multiplication

Directions: Follow along with your instructor to complete this lesson.

A. Repeated Addition (same addends)			B. Repeated Multiplication (same factors)		
0 + 0 = _____	4 + 4 = _____	8 + 8 = _____	0 x 0 = _____	4 x 4 = _____	8 x 8 = _____
1 + 1 = _____	5 + 5 = _____	9 + 9 = _____	1 x 1 = _____	5 x 5 = _____	9 x 9 = _____
2 + 2 = _____	6 + 6 = _____	10 + 10 = _____	2 x 2 = _____	6 x 6 = _____	10 x 10 = _____
3 + 3 = _____	7 + 7 = _____		3 x 3 = _____	7 x 7 = _____	

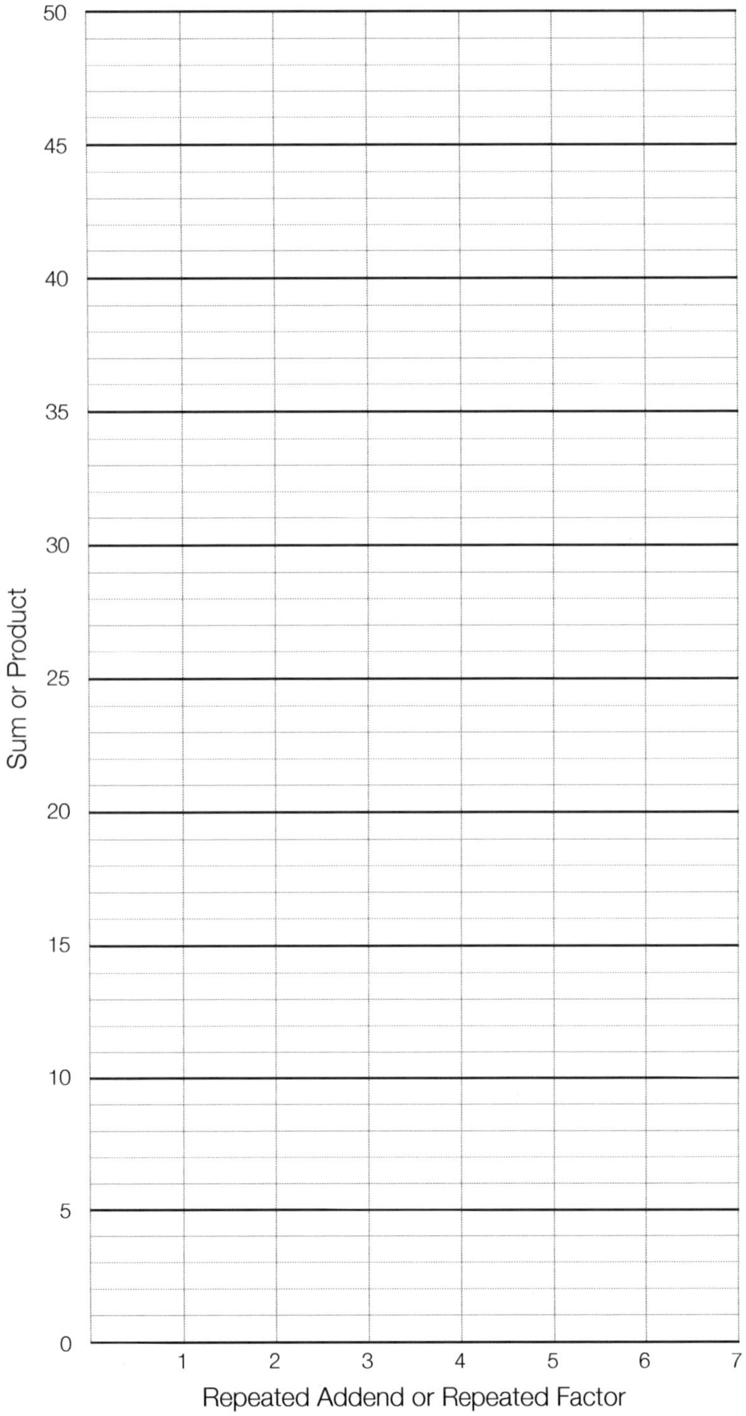

With repeated multiplication, numbers can become __________ ___________ (or __________ ______________) __________ _________________.

Use an ______________________ as a shortcut for writing repeated multiplication.

Simplify each repeated multiplication problem below using exponents.

8 x 8 x 8 = ______

3 x 3 x 3 x 3 x 3 = ______

5 x 5 x 5 x 5 x 5 = ______

Below are ***Squares*** that you've already memorized. Simplify using exponents.

5 x 5 = ______

6 x 6 = ______

7 x 7 = ______

8 x 8 = ______

A number or unit raised to the second power has been ***"squared."***

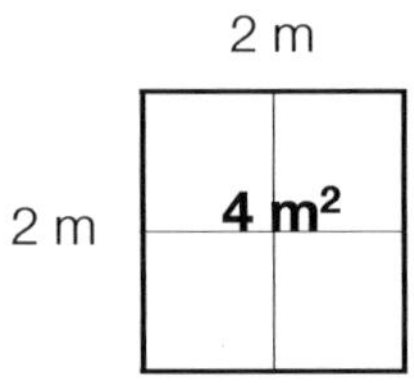

KEY LESSON

Name________________________________

Lesson 3: Exponents (1, 10, Fractions, and Integers as Bases)

Part 1: Follow along with your instructor. Expand each exponent to show repeated multiplication, then evaluate.

A. 3^2	B. 3^3	C. Use parentheses to help you. 3^4
D. 1^2	E. 1^3	F. 1^4
G. 10^2	H. 10^3	I. 10^4

Part 2: Follow along with your instructor. Expand, evaluate, then shade in the correct fraction of each circle.

J. $\left(\frac{1}{2}\right)^2$ 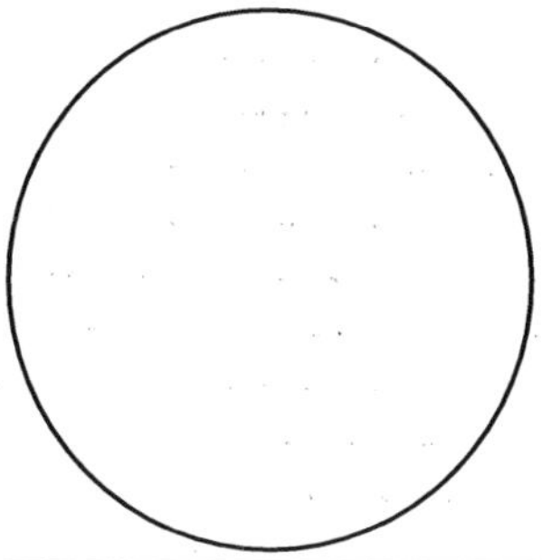	K. $\left(\frac{1}{2}\right)^3$ 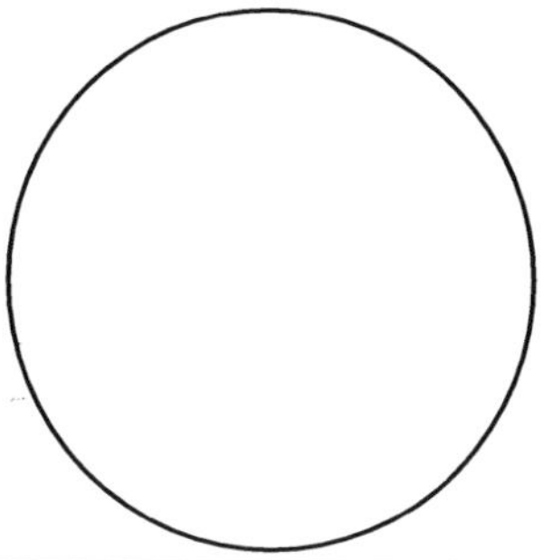	L. $\left(\frac{1}{2}\right)^4$ 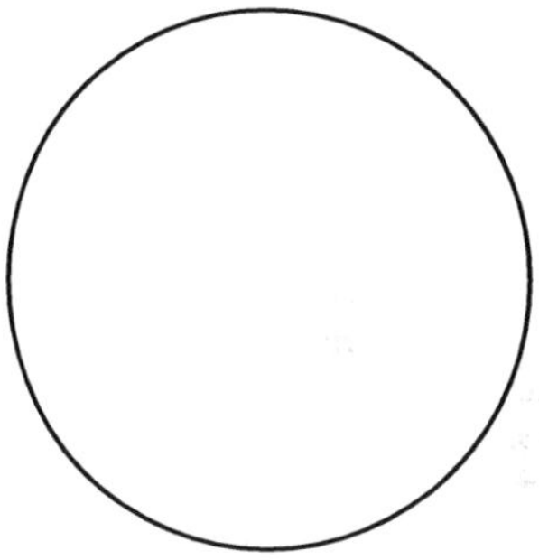

Part 3: Expand, then evaluate. In problems P, Q, R, S, T, and U, write whether your answer is ***positive*** or ***negative.***

M. $\left(\frac{2}{3}\right)^2$	N. $\left(\frac{2}{3}\right)^3$	O. $\left(\frac{2}{3}\right)^4$
P. "negative three" squared $(-3)^2$	Q. $(-3)^3$	R. $(-3)^4$
S. negative "three squared" -3^2	T. -3^3	U. -3^4

KEY LESSON

Name______________________________

Lesson 4: Exponential Growth

Directions: Follow along with your instructor to solve the following word problems.

A. Bacterial Growth

At 8:00 a.m., there was a single bacterium on a petri dish. A scientist noticed that the number of bacteria grew exponentially, ***doubling*** every hour. How many bacteria cells will there be at each of the times shown below?

_____ _____ _____ _____ _____

- Use arrows to show how to ***multiply by 2*** to find how many bacteria cells there were each hour.
- Use arrows to show how to ***divide by 2*** to find how many bacteria cells there were in the previous hour.

B. Viral Videos

The number of people who viewed a video online grew exponentially. On Sunday, one person viewed the video. Each day after that, ***four times*** as many people viewed the video compared to the day before. Complete the chart to show many people viewed the video each day of the first week. Complete the entire column titled *"Base and Exponent"* first. Note: Lesson 12 (Dividing Variables with Exponents) will further explain why $4^0 = 1$.

Day	Base and Exponent	Views
Sunday	4^0	1
Monday	4^1	4
Tuesday	4^2	16
Wednesday		
Thursday		
Friday		
Saturday		

Workspace:

- Use arrows to show how to ***multiply by 4*** to find how many views there were each day.
- Use arrows to show how to ***divide by 4*** to find how many views there were the previous day.

Name_______________________________

Lesson 5: Single-Elimination Tournament

In a single-elimination tournament, two teams at a time play against each other in a bracket. The winner of the bracket moves on to the next round, and the loser is eliminated from the tournament. After all the rounds are completed, the only team that is left is the champion.

Part 1: Exponents are used to determine how many teams to include in the tournament. With your instructor, complete the chart below. Complete the entire column titled *"Expand to Show Repeated Multiplication"* first.

Number of Rounds	Base and Exponent	Expand to Show Repeated Multiplication	Number of Teams Invited to Tournament
1	2^1		
2	2^2		
3	2^3		

Part 2: Label each round of the tournament. (Hint: The first round has 8 teams, so it is called the "Round of 8.") Then, use the game information at the bottom of the page to complete the tournament bracket, including scores.

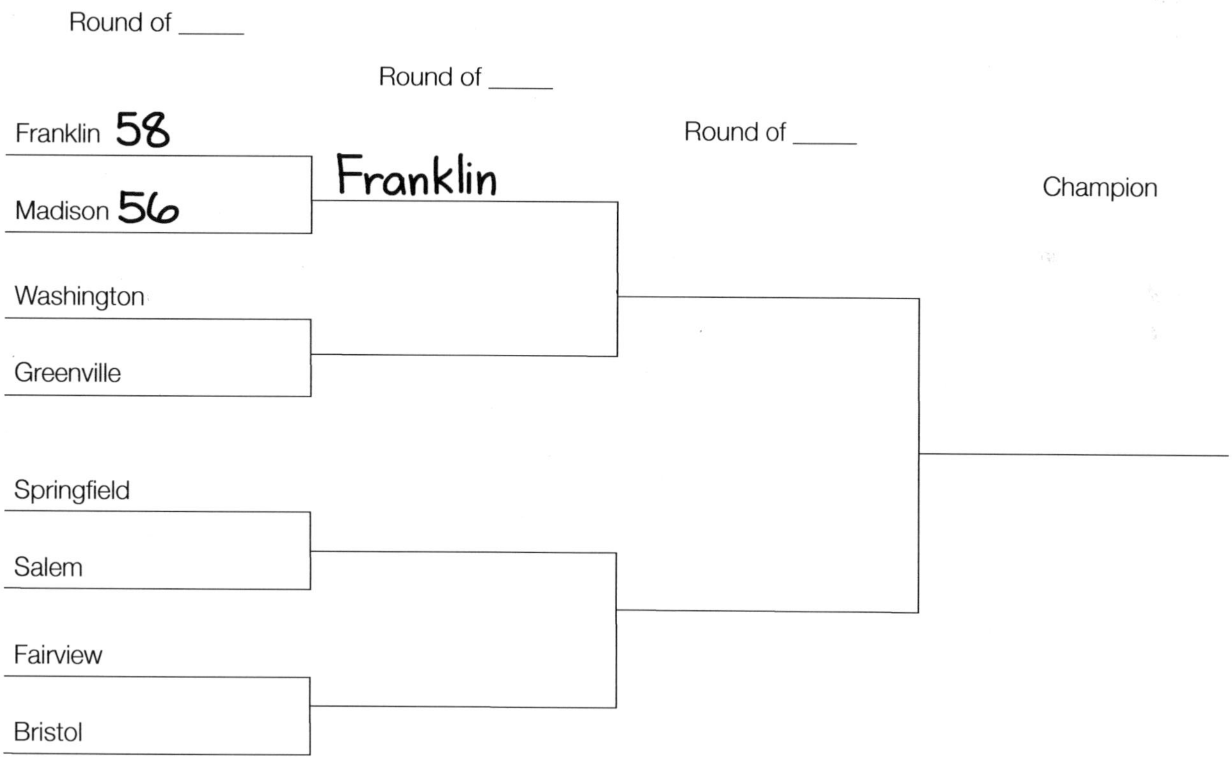

Game 1: Franklin 58, Madison 56

Game 2: Washington 63, Greenville 75

Game 3: Springfield 53, Salem 48

Game 4: Fairview 72, Bristol 75

Game 5: Franklin 65, Greenville 68

Game 6: Springfield 49, Bristol 53

Game 7: Greenville 58, Bristol 57

Name____

Lesson 6: The National Championship Tournament

Directions: In the past, a single-elimination tournament with six rounds has been used to determine the national champion in the sport of basketball. Complete the chart to find out how many teams were invited to the tournament. Complete the entire column titled *"Base and Exponent"* first.

Number of Rounds	Base and Exponent	Repeated Multiplication	Number of Teams Invited to Tournament
1	2^1	2	
2	2^2	2 x 2	
3			
4			
5			
6			

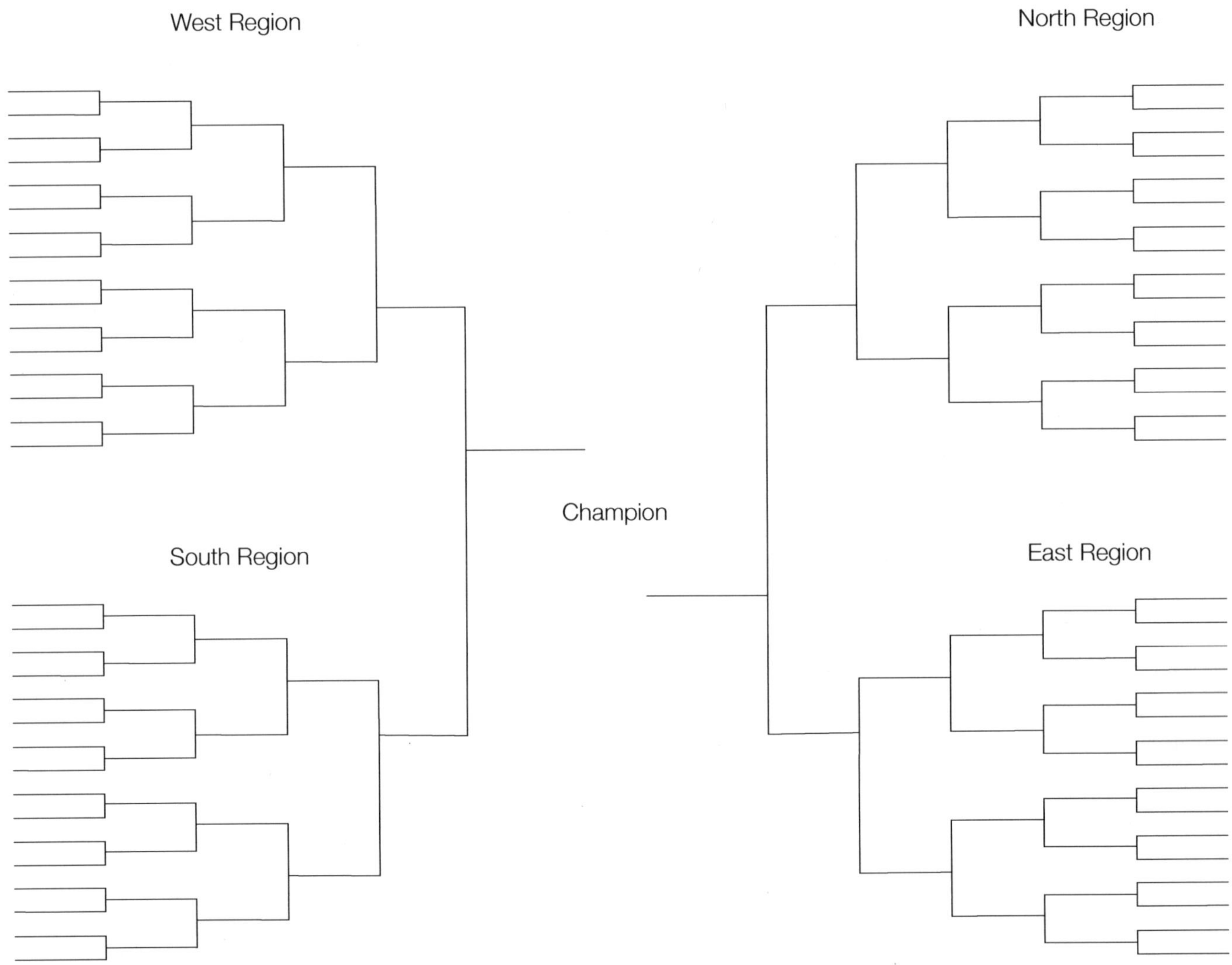

Name________________________________

Lesson 7: Adding and Subtracting Variables with Exponents

You learned earlier that you can only add and subtract fractions if they have the same name (denominator). Likewise, you can only ***add*** and ***subtract*** variables with exponents if *they* have the same name (base and exponent) as well.

Part 1: Follow along with your instructor to complete this lesson.

A. 1 apple +1 apple	B. 5 pencils −2 pencils	C. 1 fifth +2 fifths	D. 1 half +1 third
E. $3xy$ $+2xy$	F. $9x^2$ $-5x^2$	G. $4m^2n$ $+2m^2n$	H. $2mn$ $+3m^2n$

Part 2: Simplify. Use parentheses to group terms with the same base and exponent together (think "apples plus apples").

I. $x^2 + 2x + 3x + 6$	J. $x^2 + 4x - 7x - 28$	K. $x^2 + 3x + 4x + 12$	L. $x^2 + 8x + 2x + 16$
M. $y^2 + 5y + 6y + 30$	N. $y^2 + 9y - 3y - 27$	O. $y^2 + 6y + 4y + 24$	P. $y^2 + 7y + 2y + 14$

Q. $a^3 + 2a^2 + 4a^2 + 2a + 3a + 6$	R. $4a^3 + a^2 + a^2 + 2a + 3a + 8$ Careful! Hidden coefficients!
S. $b^3 + 2b^3 + 2b^2 + 8b^2 + b + 3b + 14$	T. $b^3 + b^3 + b^2 + b^2 + b + 3b + 21$

Name________________________________

Lesson 8: Adding and Subtracting Variables with Exponents

You learned earlier that you can only add and subtract fractions if they have the same name (denominator). Likewise, you can only ***add*** and ***subtract*** variables with exponents if *they* have the same name (base and exponent) as well.

Part 2: Simplify. Use parentheses to group terms with the same base and exponent together (think "apples plus apples").

A. $x^2 + 2x + 3x + 6$	B. $x^2 + 4x - 5x - 20$ Rewrite "–1x" as just "–x."	C. $n^2 + 4n + 3n + 12$	D. $n^2 + 6n + 7n + 42$
E. $y^2 + 8y - 8y - 64$ Omit "–0y" from your answer.	F. $y^2 + 7y + 8y + 56$	G. $a^2 + 5a + 6a + 30$	H. $a^2 + 5a - 3a - 15$

Part 2: Simplify. Use parentheses to group terms with the same base and exponent together (think "apples plus apples").

I. $n^3 + 4n^2 + n^2 + 2n + n + 6$ Careful! Hidden coefficients!	J. $4n^3 + n^3 + n^2 + n^2 + 3n + 8$
K. $z^3 + z^3 + 2z^2 + 8z + z + 3z + 4$	L. $z^3 + 2z^3 + z^2 + 2z^2 + 3z + z + 4$
M. $a^3 + a^3 + a^3 + a^2 + 4a^2 + a + 8$	N. $5a^3 + a^3 + 4a^2 + 2a^2 + a + 3a + 26$
O. $b^4 + b^4 + b^3 + b^3 + 2b + b + 6$	P. $b^4 + 3b^4 + 2b^3 + b^3 + b^2 + b^2 + b + 14$

KEY LESSON

Lesson 9: Multiplying Binomials

Monomial: A single term such as 5xy that involves only one name. The Latin root "nom" means "name."
Think: The term "5 apples" involves only the single name of "apples".

Polynomial: An expression with more than one term summed such as ($5xy + 3x^2y$) that involves more than one name.
Think: The summed expression (5 apples + 3 bananas) involves two names — "apples" and "bananas."

Binomial: A polynomial with exactly two terms summed such as ($5xy + 3x^2y$) that involves two names.
Think: A bicycle has two wheels. A binomial has two terms (names).

Part 1: Follow along with your instructor to complete this lesson.

A. Standard Algorithm	B. Solve the problem to the left by using an expanded approach. Expand 23 into (20 + 3), expand 22 into (20 + 2), then multiply using the same order as the standard algorithm.
2 3 x 2 2	
C. Expanded Notation	**D. Solve the problem to the left by drawing an area model.**
2 3 x 2 2 2 x 3 2 x 20 20 x 3 20 x 20 Sum	

Part 2: Multiply the binomials. All products will be polynomials and will have an exponent.

E.	F.	G.
(n + 3) x(n + 2)	(n + 4) x(n + 5)	(n + 4) x(n + 3)

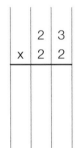

Name________________________________

Lesson 10: Multiplying Binomials

Directions: Multiply.

Big Bad Numbers

6 x 6 =	7 x 7 =	8 x 8 =	9 x 9 =
6 x 7 =	7 x 8 =	8 x 9 =	
6 x 8 =	7 x 9 =		
6 x 9 =			

Magic Triangle

A. $(n + 6)$ $\underline{\times\ (n + 8)}$	B. $(n + 6)$ $\underline{\times\ (n + 7)}$	C. $(n + 6)$ $\underline{\times\ (n + 5)}$
D. $(n + 6)$ $\underline{\times\ (n - 9)}$	E. $(n - 7)$ $\underline{\times\ (n - 7)}$	F. $(n + 8)$ $\underline{\times\ (n - 8)}$
G. Rewrite vertically, then multiply. $(a + 7)(a + 9)$	H. $(a + 8)(a + 8)$	I. $(a + 8)(a + 9)$
J. $(b + 9)(b - 7)$	K. $(b + 6)(b - 6)$	L. $(b + 5)(b + 5)$

KEY LESSON

Name______________________________

Lesson 11: Multiplying Variables with Exponents

Part 1: Expand.

A. y^3	B. y^4	C. x^4	D. x^5

Part 2: Expand, multiply, and simplify. Then, look for the shortcut.

E. $a^3 \cdot a^3$	F. $b^2 \cdot b^3$	G. $c^5 \cdot c$ Careful! Hidden exponent!	H. $d \cdot d^3$

Part 3: Simplify without expanding.

I. $j^4 \cdot j^5$	J. $d^7 \cdot d^3$	K. $e^5 \cdot e$	L. $x^2 \cdot y^3$ Careful! Different bases!
M. $x \cdot x$	N. $k^4 \cdot m^6$	O. $a \cdot a^3$	P. $a^3 \cdot a^2 \cdot a$
Q. $n^4 \cdot n^6 \cdot n^3$	R. $n^1 \cdot n^2$	S. $n^a \cdot n^b$ The bases are the same, so you can still simplify by adding the exponents (a + b).	T. $n^c \cdot n^d$

KEY LESSON

Name______________________

Lesson 12: Dividing Variables with Exponents

Part 1: Expand.

A. g^3	B. x^4	C. m^5	D. z^6

Part 2: Expand, divide, and simplify. Then, look for the shortcut.

E. $\frac{n^5}{n^3}$	F. $\frac{x^5}{x^4}$	G. $\frac{4^5}{4^3}$	H. $\frac{4^5}{4^5}$

Part 3: Simplify without expanding. Keep the base, then subtract the exponents.

I. $\frac{a^8}{a^3}$	J. $\frac{b^5}{b^2}$	K. $\frac{p^5}{p}$	L. $\frac{4^5}{4^5}$ Problem H and Problem L show that $4^0 = 1$. A base raised to the zero power equals 1.
M. $\frac{d^5}{e^3}$ Careful! Different bases!	N. $\frac{5^{100}}{5^{98}}$	O. $\frac{2^9}{2^9}$	P. $\frac{j^{75}}{j^{25}}$
Q. $\frac{k^5m^2}{k^3}$	R. $\frac{x^5y^4}{y^2}$	S. $\frac{x^3y^4}{x}$	T. $\frac{x^6y^3}{x^2y}$

KEY LESSON

Name________________________________

Lesson 13: Dividing Variables with Exponents (Negative Exponents)

Part 1: Expand.

A. h^2	B. y^5	C. n^4	D. r^2

Part 2: The first row and the second row use the exact same problems, but they will be simplified in two different ways.

- In the ***first row*** (E1, F1, G1, and H1), expand, then simplify each fraction.
- In the ***second row*** (E2, F2, G2, and H2), divide by keeping the base and subtracting the exponents.

E1. Expand, divide, and simplify. $\frac{p^3}{p^5}$	F1. Expand, divide, and simplify. $\frac{q^3}{q^6}$	G1. Expand, divide, and simplify. $\frac{r^2}{r^5}$	H1. Expand, divide, and simplify. $\frac{s^2}{s^6}$
E2. Subtract the exponents. $\frac{p^3}{p^5}$	F2. Subtract the exponents. $\frac{q^3}{q^6}$	G2. Subtract the exponents. $\frac{r^2}{r^5}$	H2. Subtract the exponents. $\frac{s^2}{s^6}$

Part 3: Divide by subtracting the exponents. ***For problems Q, R, S, and T, take care of one base at a time.***

I. $\frac{w^7}{w^6}$	J. $\frac{x^7}{x^2}$	K. $\frac{y}{y^4}$	L. $\frac{z^5}{x^3}$ Careful! Different bases!
M. $\frac{a^6}{a}$	N. $\frac{b^{100}}{b^{97}}$	O. $\frac{c^{11}}{c^{12}}$	P. $\frac{d^{75}}{d^{100}}$
Q. Simplify base e, then base g. $\frac{e^3g^2}{e^4}$	R. $\frac{h^5j^2}{j^5}$	S. $\frac{km^4}{k^5}$	T. $\frac{n^7p}{n^2p^3}$

KEY LESSON

Name______________________________

Lesson 14: Multiplying Variables with Exponents (Negative Exponents)

Part 1: Add the integers.

A. $5 + -2 =$ ______	B. $-5 + 2 =$ ______	C. $-5 + -2 =$ ______	D. $-5 + -6 =$ ______

Part 2: Rewrite using fractions instead of using negative exponents. Refer to Lesson 13, Part 2.

E. $a^{-2} =$	F. $b^{-5} =$	G. $c^{-4} =$	H. $d^{-5} =$

Part 3: Simplify. Two of the answers will have negative exponents.

I. $a^5a^{-2} =$	J. $b^7b^{-6} =$	K. $c^4c^{-7} =$	L. $d^{-5}d^{-2} =$

Part 4: Simplify. ***Rewrite terms with negative exponents as fractions.***

M. $w^6\,w^{-4}$	N. $w^{-6}\,w^4$	O. $w^{-6}\,w^{-4}$	P. $w^6\,c^{-4}$ Careful! Different bases!
Q. $x^{-3}\,x^8$	R. $x^{-3}\,x^{-8}$	S. $x^3\,m^{-8}$	T. $x^3\,x^{-8}$
U. $(rst)^{-2}\,(rst)^{-3}$	V. $(rst)^2\,(rst)^3$	W. $(rst)^2\,(rst)^{-3}$	X. $(rst)^{-2}\,(rst)^3$

Name______________________________

Lesson 15: Multiplying and Dividing Variables with Exponents

Part 1: Simplify.

A. $x \cdot x$	B. $j \cdot j^3$	C. $d^7 \cdot d$	D. $k^4 \cdot m^6$ Careful! Different bases!
E. $g^{10} \cdot g^{10}$	F. $e^5 \cdot e$	G. $n^4 \cdot n^3 \cdot n^2$	H. $b^2 \cdot b^3$
I. $10^4 \cdot 10$ Leave in exponential form.	J. $10^2 \cdot 10^2 \cdot 10^2$ Leave in exponential form.	K. $10^a \cdot 10^b$	L. $k^c \cdot m^d$

Part 2: Simplify.

M. $\frac{j^{10}}{j^4}$	N. $\frac{c^5}{c}$	O. $\frac{b^5}{b^2}$	P. $\frac{d^5}{e^3}$ Careful! Different bases!
Q. $\frac{10^8}{10^2}$ Leave in exponential form.	R. $\frac{10^5}{10}$ Leave in exponential form.	S. $\frac{h^9}{x^5}$	T. $\frac{3^2}{5^2}$ Leave in exponential form.
U. $\frac{x^5y^4}{x^2}$	V. $\frac{x^3y^4}{x}$	W. $\frac{x^4y^4}{x^2y}$	X. $\frac{k^5m^2}{k^3m}$

Name________________________________

Lesson 16: Multiplying and Dividing Variables with Exponents

Part 1: Simplify. ***Rewrite terms with negative exponents as fractions.*** Be careful of bases that are different.

A. $a^5\ a^{-4}$	B. $a^{-5}\ a^4$	C. $a^{-5}\ a^{-4}$	D. $a^5\ a^4$
E. $\frac{a^5}{a^4}$	F. $\frac{a^4}{a^5}$	G. $\frac{a^5}{a^5}$	H. $a^{-5}\ b^4$

Part 2: Evaluate. Remember that a base raised to the zero power equals 1.

I. $2^{-4} \cdot 2^2$	J. $\frac{2^4}{2^4}$	K. $2^2 \cdot 2^4$	L. $\frac{2^4}{2}$
M. $\frac{2^2}{2^4}$	N. $2^{-2} \cdot 2^4$	O. $2^{-4} \cdot 2^{-2}$	P. $\frac{2}{2^4}$

Part 3: Simplify. ***Rewrite terms with negative exponents as fractions.*** Be careful of bases that are different.

Q. $(de)^{-10}\ (de)^5$	R. $\frac{(de)^{10}}{(de)^5}$	S. $(de)^5\ (fg)^{-10}$	T. $\frac{(de)^5}{(de)}$
U. $\frac{(de)^{10}}{(de)^{10}}$	V. $(de)^{-5}\ (de)^{10}$	W. $(de)^{-10}\ (de)^{-5}$	X. $\frac{(de)}{(de)^5}$

KEY LESSON

Name________________________________

Lesson 17: Comparing Numbers with Exponents

Part 1: Evaluate.

A. 2^1	B. 5^1	C. 24^1
D. 2^0	E. 5^0	F. 37^0
G. 1^3	H. 1^5	I. 1^{100}
J. Use parentheses to help you. 3^4	K. 4^5	L. Use parentheses and Box K to help you. 2^{10}
M. $(-4)^2$	N. -4^2	O. $-(4^2)$

Part 2: Use the symbols greater than (>), less than (<), or equal to (=) to compare exponents. Use the white space to show your work. Remember that a base raised to the zero power equals 1.

P. 2^3 ____ 3^2	Q. 2^4 ____ 4^2	R. 2^5 ____ 5^2
S. Use Box J to help you. 3^4 ____ 4^3	T. Use Box L to help you. 2^{10} ____ 10^2	U. Use Box L and Box K to help you. 2^{10} ____ 4^5
V. 1^{100} ____ 100^1	W. 5^0 ____ 37^0	X. 0^0 ____ 1^0
Y. $(-4)^2$ ____ -4^2	Z. -4^2 ____ $-(4^2)$	AA. $-(4^2)$ ____ $(-4)^2$

KEY LESSON

Name________________________________

Lesson 18: Scientific Notation

Part 1: Follow along with your instructor to complete this lesson. Expand and evaluate.

A. 10^2	B. 10^3	C. Evaluate without expanding. 10^6	D. Evaluate without expanding. 10^5

Part 2: Rewrite these ***powers of ten*** using exponents.

E. 1,000	F. 100	G. 100,000	H. 1,000,000

Part 3: Factor into a single-digit number times a power of ten. Then, write that power of ten using an exponent.

Example: 700 $=7 \times 100$ $=7 \times 10^2$	I. 9,000	J. 3,000,000	K. 6,000,000,000,000 Go straight to the answer without factoring.

Part 4: Circle the number that is not written in normalized scientific notation. Explain why it is not in scientific notation.

L. 8.3×10^3 7.2×10^5 13.4×10^4 3.6×10^7	M. 4.2×10^6 1.7×8^3 3.9×10^2 5.6×10^5	N. 3.335×10^8 4.2623×10^3 0.2623×10^9 3.35×10^6	O. 4.7×10^{-8} 3.8×10^{-9} 6.5×10^{-5} 12.3×10^{-2}

Part 5: Write each number in scientific notation without factoring first. Target your new decimal point FIRST.

P. 1,345	Q. 3,250,000	R. Notice the decimal point! 103,000.00	S. Notice the decimal point! 467,300,000.0
T. .00023	U. .00000594	V. 0.0000001	W. 0.00058

Name________________________

Lesson 19: Scientific Notation

Part 1: Evaluate.

A. 8.3×10^3	B. 7.2×10^5	C. 3.35×10^6	D. 4.2623×10^3
E. 1.23×10^2	F. 6.5×10^5	G. 3.8×10^4	H. 4.732×10^2

Part 2: Evaluate. All of these problems contain negative exponents.

I. 1.23×10^{-2}	J. 6.5×10^{-5}	K. 3.8×10^{-4}	L. 4.732×10^{-2}

Part 3: Write in scientific notation. Target your new decimal point first.

M. 1,350	N. 1,350,000	O. 13,500,000.0	P. 135,000,000.0
Q. 0.135	R. 0.0000135	S. 0.0135	T. 0.00000000135

Part 4: Write in scientific notation. Target your new decimal point first.

U. 275,000	V. 4,850,000	W. 9,000,000	X. 25,250,000
Y. 0.509	Z. 0.00509	AA. 0.051	AB. 0.0000000401

Name________________________________

Lesson 20: Exponents Review

Part 1: Add or subtract.

A. $\begin{array}{r} 6xy \\ \underline{+4xy} \end{array}$	B. $\begin{array}{r} 8x^2 \\ \underline{-3x^2} \end{array}$	C. $\begin{array}{r} 5m^2n \\ \underline{-2m^2n} \end{array}$	D. $\begin{array}{r} 4mn \\ \underline{+3m^2n} \end{array}$

Part 2: Simplify. Rewrite terms with negative exponents as fractions. ***Leave problems G and L in exponential form.***

E. $a^6 a^{-4}$	F. $(xyz)^{-6} (xyz)^4$	G. $23^{-6} 23^{-4}$	H. $h^6 w^{-4}$
I. $\frac{b^5}{b^3}$	J. $\frac{b^3}{b^5}$	K. $\frac{c^5d^7}{c^5d^3}$	L. $\frac{15^7 23^6}{15^2 23^8}$

Part 3: Evaluate.

M. 4.25×10^6	N. 7.3245×10^3	O. 9.8×10^{-4}	P. 5.632×10^{-2}

Part 4: Write each number in scientific notation. Target your new decimal point FIRST.

Q. 365,000	R. 7,950,000	S. 0.00409	T. 0.081

Name________________________________

Lesson 21: Exponents Review

Part 1: Add or subtract.

A. $\begin{array}{r} 7abc \\ \underline{-3abc} \end{array}$	B. $\begin{array}{r} 9y^2 \\ \underline{+2y^2} \end{array}$	C. $\begin{array}{r} 4c^2d \\ \underline{-3c^2d} \end{array}$	D. $\begin{array}{r} 5m^2n \\ \underline{+6m^2n} \end{array}$

Part 2: Simplify. Rewrite terms with negative exponents as fractions. ***Leave problems G and L in exponential form.***

E. $w^3 w^{-8}$	F. $(abc)^{-4} (abc)^2$	G. $3^{-4} 3^{-2}$	H. $m^6 m^{-4}$
I. $\frac{n^9}{n^7}$	J. $\frac{n^7}{n^9}$	K. $\frac{r^5s^3}{r^4s^8}$	L. $\frac{25^4 43^6}{25^2 43^9}$

Part 3: Evaluate.

M. 6.25×10^5	N. 8.3445×10^2	O. 8.4×10^{-3}	P. 3.141×10^{-3}

Part 4: Write each number in scientific notation. Target your new decimal point FIRST.

Q. 525,600	R. 5,150,000	S. 0.00405	T. 0.042

KEY LESSON

Name____

Lesson 22: Diamond Puzzles

Part 1: Follow along with your instructor to complete this lesson. Factor.

A. 12	B. 16	C. 18	D. 20
___ · ___	___ · ___	___ · ___	___ · ___
___ · ___	___ · ___	___ · ___	___ · ___
___ · ___	___ · ___	___ · ___	___ · ___

Part 2: Solve each puzzle by finding the two numbers whose ***product*** is equal to the number at the top of the diamond and whose ***sum*** is equal to the number at the bottom of the diamond. The solution for the example is 6 and 2 because 6 x 2 = 12 and 6 + 2 = 8.

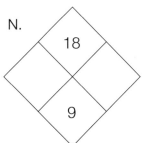

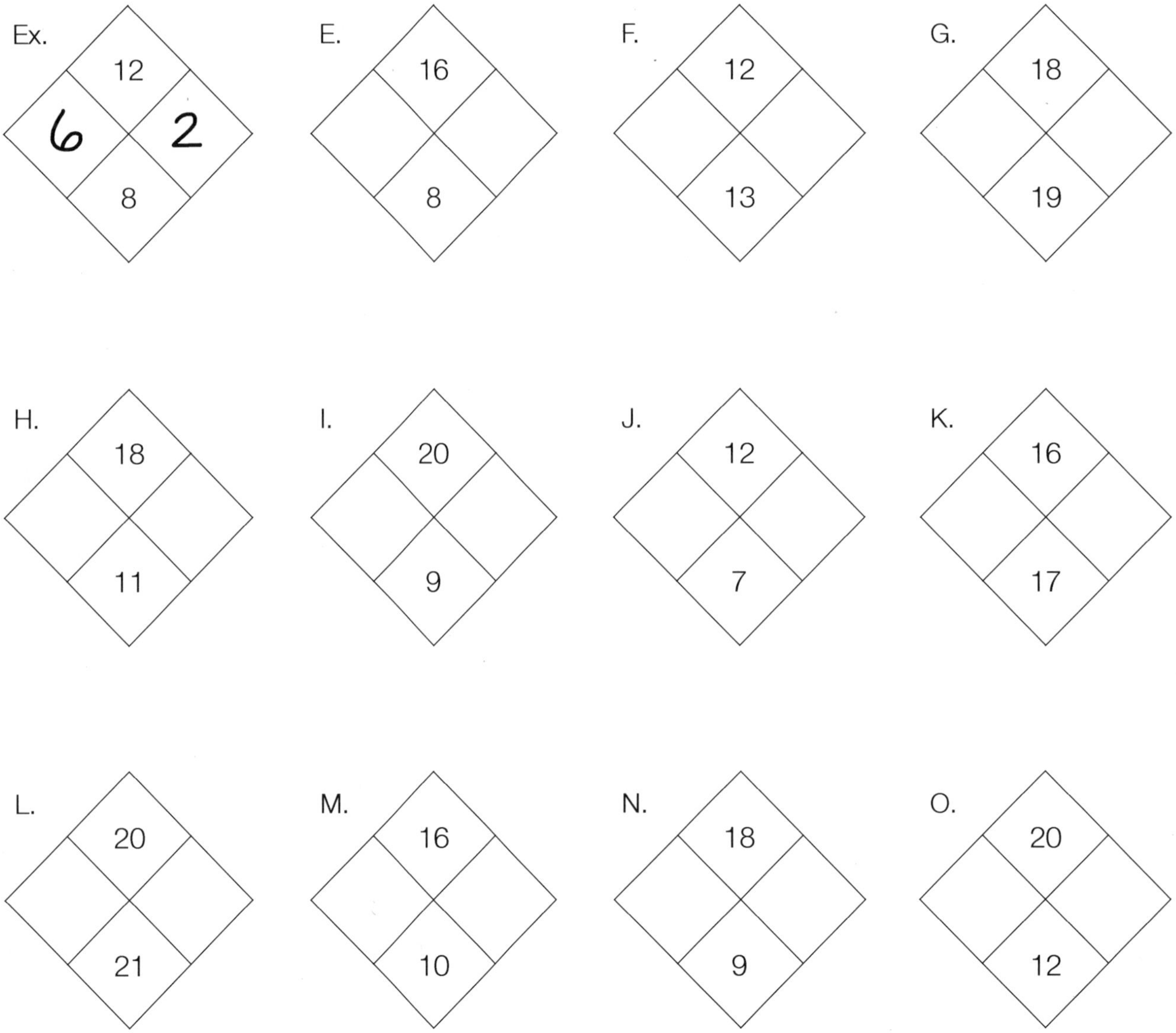

KEY LESSON

Name________________________________

Lesson 23: Factoring Quadratic Expressions

Quadratic: Involving a base raised to the second power (squares) and no higher power.
The Latin word "quadratus" means "square."

Part 1: Follow along with your instructor to complete this lesson. Write the following ***squares*** using exponents.

A.			B.		
1 x 1 = 1^2	4 x 4 = _____	7 x 7 = _____	n · n = _____	a · a = _____	r · r = _____
2 x 2 = _____	5 x 5 = _____	8 x 8 = _____	x · x = _____	b · b = _____	s · s = _____
3 x 3 = _____	6 x 6 = _____	9 x 9 = _____	y · y = _____	c · c = _____	d · d = _____

Part 2: Factor.

C. 12	D. 16	E. 18	F. 20
___ · ___	___ · ___	___ · ___	___ · ___
___ · ___	___ · ___	___ · ___	___ · ___
___ · ___	___ · ___	___ · ___	___ · ___

Part 3: With your instructor, use the diamond puzzle in Box G to factor the quadratic expression $n^2 + 7n + 12$ in Box H. Then, check your work by multiplying the factors in Box I.

G. Solve the diamond puzzle.

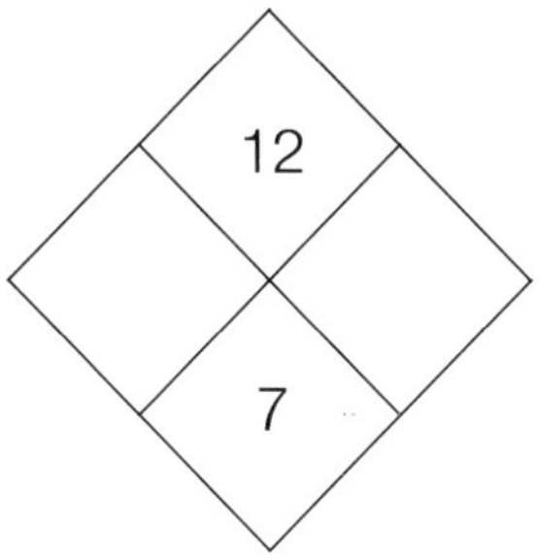

H. Factor.

$n^2 + 7n + 12$

I. Multiply to check your answer.

Part 4: Factor the quadratic expressions. Use the hint if necessary.

J.

$n^2 + 10n + 16$

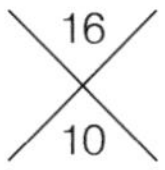

K.

$n^2 + 9n + 20$

L.

$n^2 + 21n + 20$

Name____

Lesson 24: Diamond Puzzles

Part 1: Solve each problem.

A. List the factors of 63.	B.	C.
___ · ___	63 + 1 = _____	63 – 1 = _____
___ · ___	9 + 7 = _____	9 – 7 = _____

Part 2: Solve each puzzle by finding the two numbers whose ***product*** is equal to the number at the top of the diamond and whose ***sum*** is equal to the number at the bottom of the diamond. Use Boxes A, B, and C above to help you. The solution for the example is –9 and 7 because –9 x 7 = –63 and –9 + 7 = –2.

Ex.
–63
–2

D.
63
16

E.
–63
2

F.
63
–16

G.
63
64

H.
63
–64

I.
–63
–62

J.
–63
62

K.
15
8

L.
15
–8

M.
15
–16

N.
15
16

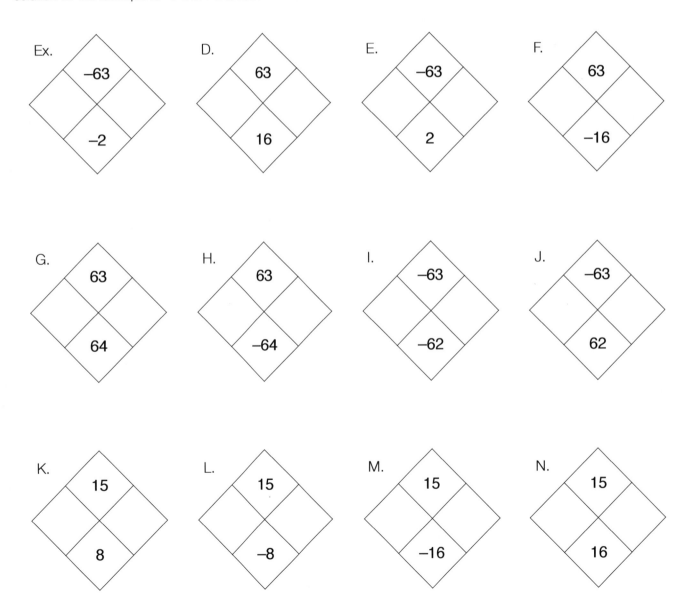

Name________________________________

Lesson 25: Factoring Quadratic Expressions

Part 1: Solve each problem.

A. List the factors of 63. ___ · ___ ___ · ___	B. 63 + 1 = _____ 9 + 7 = _____	C. 63 – 1 = _____ 9 – 7 = _____

Part 2: Factor the quadratic expressions in ***Row 1.*** Then, use multiplication in ***Row 2*** to check your work.

D1. $x^2 + 64x + 63$ 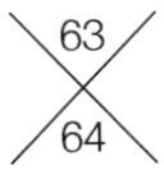 	E1. $x^2 + 16x + 15$	F1. $x^2 + 16x + 63$
D2. Multiply to check your answer above.	E2. Multiply to check your answer above.	F2. Multiply to check your answer above.

Part 3: Factor the quadratic expressions in ***Row 1.*** Then, use multiplication in ***Row 2*** to check your work.

G1. $n^2 - 2n - 63$ 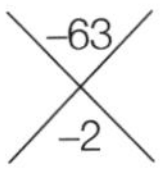 	H1. $n^2 + 2n - 63$	I1. $n^2 - 64n + 63$
G2. Multiply to check your answer above.	H2. Multiply to check your answer above.	I2. Multiply to check your answer above.

KEY LESSON

Name____________________

Lesson 26: Factoring Quadratic Expressions to Simplify Fractions

Part 1: Follow along with your instructor to complete this lesson. Factor, then simplify.

A.

$$\frac{x^2 + 8x + 12}{x^2 + 14x + 48}$$

B.

$$\frac{n^2 + 9n + 20}{n^2 + 10n + 25}$$

C.

$$\frac{a^2 + 12a + 36}{a^2 + 8a + 12}$$

D.

$$\frac{m^2 + 17m + 72}{m + 4 + 4}$$

Part 2: Factor, simplify, then multiply.

E.

$$\frac{n^2 + 10n + 21}{n^2 + 9n + 20} \cdot \frac{n^2 + 6n + 8}{n^2 + 5n + 6}$$

F.

$$\frac{y^2 + 8y + 15}{y^2 + 7y + 12} \cdot \frac{y^2 + 6y + 8}{y^2 + 7y + 10}$$

KEY LESSON

Name________________________________

Lesson 27: Using the Distributive Property to Multiply Polynomials

Part 1: Follow along with your instructor to complete this lesson.

A. Standard Algorithm 1 3 4 x 2 _____	B. Solve the problem to the left by expanding 134 into (100 + 30 + 4) and multiplying every term in the parentheses by 2.
C. Expanded Notation 1 3 4 x 2 _____ 2 x 4 2 x 30 2 x 100 Sum	D. Solve the problem to the left by drawing an area model.

Part 2: Use the distributive property to multiply.

E. $(s^2 + 5s + 6)$ $\cdot s$	F. $(t^2 + 7t + 10)$ $\cdot 7$	G. $(u^2 + 5u + 6)$ $\cdot 5u$

Part 3: Use the distributive property to multiply horizontally. Do not rewrite the problems vertically.

Example: $2(100 + 30 + 4)$ $= 200 + 60 + 8$ $= 268$	H. $3(200 + 40 + 3)$	I. $2(s^2 + 5s + 6)$
J. $7(t^2 + 7t + 10)$	K. $5u(u^2 + 5u + 6)$	L. $x^2(x^2 + x + 1)$

Name____

Lesson 28: Multiplying Binomials Using the FOIL Method

Part 1: Follow along with your instructor to complete this lesson. In Lessons 9 and 10, you easily multiplied binomials using vertical multiplication. Complete the problems below.

A.

	3	1
x	3	2

B.

$$\begin{array}{r} (30 + 1) \\ \underline{x(30 + 2)} \end{array}$$

C.

$$\begin{array}{r} (n + 5) \\ \underline{x(n + 6)} \end{array}$$

Part 2: You can also multiply binomials using the FOIL method. FOIL stands for **F**irst, **O**uter, **I**nner, and **L**ast. Complete the analogies below with your instructor.

D. Each tandem bicycle below has a rider who is first and a rider who is last. Label each rider on each tandem bicycle as ***"first"*** or ***"last."***

________ ________ ________ ________

E. Each set of parentheses below has a term that is first and a term that is last. Label each term in each set of parentheses as ***"first"*** or ***"last."***

________ ________ ________ ________

(n + 5) (n + 6)

F. Look at the four bicyclists all in a row. Two of them have the inner position, and two have the outer position. Label the riders ***"inner"*** or ***"outer."***

________ ________ ________ ________

G. Look at the four terms all in a row. Two of them have the inner position, and two have the outer position. Label the terms "***"inner"*** or ***"outer."***

________ ________ ________ ________

(n + 5) (n + 6)

Part 3: To use the FOIL method, multiply the **F**irst terms, the **O**uter terms, the **I**nner terms, and the **L**ast terms. Multiply (n + 5)(n + 6). Then, simplify your answer by combining terms with the same bases (think "apples plus apples").

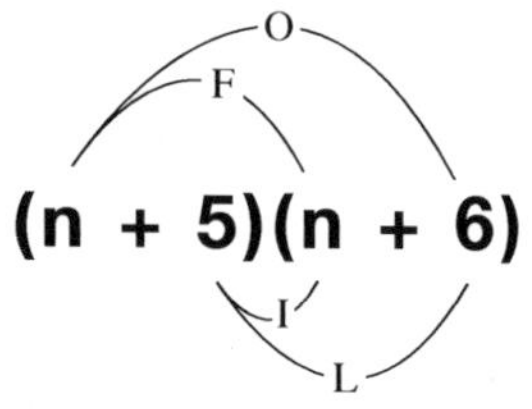

H.

(n + 5)(n + 6)

KEY LESSON

Name____

Lesson 29: Multiplying Binomials Using the FOIL Method (or the FIOL Method)

Directions: Follow along with your instructor. Multiply by using the FOIL method instead of using vertical multiplication. In each set of parentheses, multiply the **F**irst terms, the **I**nner terms, the **O**uter terms, and the **L**ast terms.

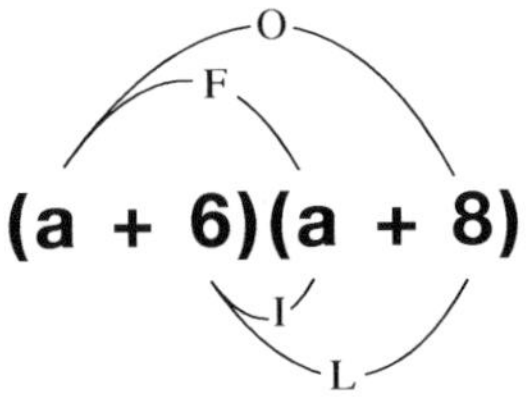

Important Note: *Visually, many students find it easier to go in this order instead:* ***F****irst,* ***I****nner,* ***O****uter,* ***L****ast.* The reason for this is that after you multiply the *First* terms, your eyes are already looking at the *Inner* terms (which are also close together), so it's more convenient to multiply the Inner terms next. Then, multiply the Outer terms and the Last terms.

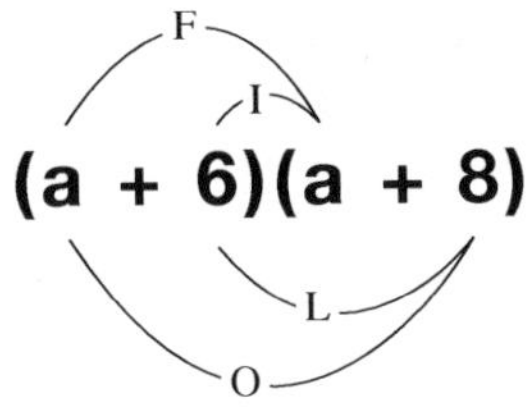

A. Try this order: **F**irst, **I**nner, **O**uter, **L**ast. $(a + 6)(a + 8)$	B. $(b + 6)(b + 9)$	C. $(c + 7)(c + 9)$
D. $(d + 6)(d + 6)$	E. $(e + 6)(e + 7)$	F. $(f + 6)(f + 5)$
G. $(g + 7)^2$	H. $(h + 8)^2$	I. $(j + 9)^2$
J. $(3k + 2)(k + 4)$	K. $(2m + 3)(m + 5)$	L. $(4n + 7)(n + 3)$

KEY LESSON

Name________________________________

Lesson 30: Multiplying Binomials Using the FOIL Method (or the FIOL Method)

Part 1: Follow along with your instructor to complete this lesson. Add, subtract, or multiply.

A.	B.	C.	D.
$3 + 5 =$ ____	$5 + 3 =$ ____	$3 \cdot 5 =$ ____	$5 \cdot 3 =$ ____
$3 - 5 =$ ____	$5 - 3 =$ ____	$3 \cdot -5 =$ ____	$5 \cdot -3 =$ ____
$-3 + 5 =$ ____	$-5 + 3 =$ ____	$-3 \cdot 5 =$ ____	$-5 \cdot 3 =$ ____
$-3 - 5 =$ ____	$-5 - 3 =$ ____	$-3 \cdot -5 =$ ____	$-5 \cdot -3 =$ ____

Part 2: Multiply using the FOIL method. *Visually, many find it easier to go in this order instead:* ***F****irst,* ***I****nner,* ***O****uter,* ***L****ast. The reason for this is that after you multiply the First terms, your eyes are already looking at the Inner terms (which are also close together), so it's more convenient to multiply the Inner terms next. Then, multiply the Outer terms and the Last terms.*

E. $(x + 3)(x + 5)$	F. $(x + 3)(x - 5)$	G. $(x -3)(x + 5)$
H. $(x - 3)(x - 5)$	I. $(x - 5)(x - 3)$	J. $(x + 5)(x + 3)$
K. $(x + 5)(x - 3)$	L. $(x - 5)(x + 3)$	M. $(x - 3)(x - 5)$

Name________________________________

Lesson 31: Multiplying Binomials Using the FOIL Method (or the FIOL Method)

Part 1: Add, subtract, or multiply.

A.	B.	C.	D.
$4 + 9 =$ ____	$9 + 4 =$ ____	$4 \cdot 9 =$ ____	$9 \cdot 4 =$ ____
$4 - 9 =$ ____	$9 - 4 =$ ____	$4 \cdot -9 =$ ____	$9 \cdot -4 =$ ____
$-4 + 9 =$ ____	$-9 + 4 =$ ____	$-4 \cdot 9 =$ ____	$-9 \cdot 4 =$ ____
$-4 - 9 =$ ____	$-9 - 4 =$ ____	$-4 \cdot -9 =$ ____	$-9 \cdot -4 =$ ____

Part 2: Multiply using the FOIL method. *Visually, many find it easier to go in this order instead: **F**irst, **I**nner, **O**uter, **L**ast. The reason for this is that after you multiply the First terms, your eyes are already looking at the Inner terms (which are also close together), so it's more convenient to multiply the Inner terms next. Then, multiply the Outer terms and the Last terms.*

E. $(x + 4)(x + 9)$	F. $(x + 4)(x - 9)$	G. $(x - 4)(x + 9)$
H. $(x - 4)(x - 9)$	I. $(x - 9)(x - 4)$	J. $(x + 9)(x + 4)$
K. $(x + 9)(x - 4)$	L. $(x - 9)(x + 4)$	M. $(x - 4)(x - 9)$

KEY LESSON

Name____

Lesson 32: Adding and Subtracting Numbers with Exponents

In previous lessons you learned the following:

- You can only add and subtract ***objects*** if they have the same name (for example, "apples plus apples").
- You can only add and subtract ***fractions*** if they have the same name (denominator).
- You can only add and subtract ***variables with exponents*** if they have the same name (base and exponent).

This same concept applies to ***numbers with exponents*** as well. If numbers do not have the same base and exponent, you'll need to evaluate them first before adding and subtracting them.

Part 1: Follow along with your instructor to complete this lesson.

A. 1 pencil +1 pencil	B. 1 plant +1 radio	C. 1 third +1 third	D. 1 half +1 third
E. $5x^2y$ $+3x^2y$	F. $5x^2y^2$ $+3x^2y$	G. 3 thousand +4 thousand	H. 3 million +4 thousand

Part 2: Simplify. Leave all your answers in exponential form. Remember that ***variables with exponents*** and ***numbers with exponents*** can only be added and subtracted if they have the same base and exponent.

I1. $a^4 + a^{-5} + a^{-5}$	J1. $b^4 + b^4 + b^4$	K1. $c^{10} + c^9 + c^9 + c^9$	L1. $d^3 + d^3 + d^3 + d^{-4}$
I2. $7^4 + 7^{-5} + 7^{-5}$	J2. $11^4 + 11^4 + 11^4$	K2. $8^{10} + 8^9 + 8^9 + 8^9$	L2. $9^3 + 9^3 + 9^3 + 9^{-4}$

M. $10^6 + 10^6 + 10^3 + 10^3 + 10^3 + 10^3 + 10^2$	N. $10^6 + 10^3 + 10^2 + 10^2 + 10^2 + 10^2 + 10^0$

KEY LESSON

Name_______________

Lesson 33: Adding, Subtracting, and Multiplying Numbers with Exponents

Part 1: Simplify. Leave your answers in exponential form.

A. Expand first, then simplify. $17^3 \cdot 17^3$	B. Simplify without expanding. $17^9 \cdot 17^{-4}$	C. Write as a fraction. $17^9 \cdot 17^{-11}$	D. Write as a fraction. $23^4 \cdot 17^{-9}$

Part 2: Simplify. Leave your answers in exponential form. Remember that ***variables with exponents*** and ***numbers with exponents*** can only be added and subtracted if they have the same base and exponent.

E. $17^4 + 17^3 + 17^3$	F. $17^9 + 17^4 + 17^4 + 17^4$	G. $17^9 + 17^9 + 17^9 + 17^9$	H. $17^9 + 17^9 + 17^9 + 17^4$

Part 3: Evaluate. Remember that a number raised to the zero power equals 1.

I. $(2^{13} \cdot 2^{-10}) + 2^4$	J. $2^3 + (2^{-3} \cdot 2^5)$	K. $(3^{25} \cdot 3^{-22}) + 3^2$	L. $3^0 + 3^{-2}$

Part 4: Evaluate. Remember that a number raised to the zero power equals 1.

M.

$10^0 =$ _____	$10^3 =$ _________	$10^6 =$ ______________
$10^1 =$ _____	$10^4 =$ _________	$10^7 =$ ______________
$10^2 =$ _____	$10^5 =$ _________	$10^8 =$ ______________

Part 5: Evaluate. Remember that a number raised to the zero power equals 1.

N. $10^6 + 10^6 + 10^3 + 10^3 + 10^3 + 10^3 + 10^0$	O. $10^6 + 10^3 + 10^2 + 10^2 + 10^2 + 10^2$

KEY LESSON

Name____

Lesson 34: Comparing Numbers with Exponents

Part 1: Expand, then evaluate. Notice the patterns that result in each row.

A. $(-2)^2$	B. $(-2)^3$	C. $(-2)^4$	D. $(-2)^5$
E. -2^2	F. -2^3	G. -2^4	H. -2^5
I. $(-2)^{-2}$	J. $(-2)^{-3}$	K. $(-2)^{-4}$	L. $(-2)^{-5}$
M. -2^{-2}	N. -2^{-3}	O. -2^{-4}	P. -2^{-5}

Pattern in Row 1 (Boxes A-D): alternating ________________ and ________________

Pattern in Row 2 (Boxes E-H): all ________________

Pattern in Row 3 (Boxes I-L): alternating ________________ and ________________ ________________

Pattern in Row 4 (Boxes M-P): all ________________ ________________

Part 2: Use the symbols greater than (>), less than (<), or equal to (=) to compare exponents. Show your work.

Q. $(-2)^2$ ____ -2^2	R. $(-2)^3$ ____ -2^3	S. -2^4 ____ $(-2)^4$
T. -2^2 ____ -2^{-2}	U. $(-2)^4$ ____ $(-2)^{-4}$	V. $(-2)^5$ ____ -2^{-5}

Name____________________________

Lesson 35: Comparing Numbers with Exponents

Part 1: Expand, then evaluate. Notice the patterns that result in each row.

A. -10^2	B. -10^3	C. -10^4	D. -10^5
E. $(-10)^2$	F. $(-10)^3$	G. $(-10)^4$	H. $(-10)^5$
I. -10^{-2}	J. -10^{-3}	K. -10^{-4}	L. -10^{-5}
M. $(-10)^{-2}$	N. $(-10)^{-3}$	O. $(-10)^{-4}$	P. $(-10)^{-5}$

Pattern in Row 1 (Boxes A-D): all ______________

Pattern in Row 2 (Boxes E-H): alternating ______________ and ______________

Pattern in Row 3 (Boxes I-L): all ______________ ______________

Pattern in Row 4 (Boxes M-P): alternating ______________ and ______________ ______________

Part 2: Use the symbols greater than (>), less than (<), or equal to (=) to compare exponents. Show your work.

Q. -10^2 ____ -10^{-2}	R. $(-10)^5$ ____ -10^{-5}	S. $(-10)^4$ ____ $(-10)^{-4}$
T. $(-10)^3$ ____ -10^3	U. $(-10)^2$ ____ -10^2	V. -10^4 ____ $(-10)^4$

KEY LESSON

Name________________________________

Lesson 36: Comparing Fractions with Exponents

Part 1: Follow along with your instructor. Expand, then evaluate. Notice the patterns from row to row.

- Row 1: **The number 1** is raised to second, third, and fourth powers.
- Row 2: **A number greater than 1** is raised to second, third, and fourth powers.
- Row 3: **A fraction** is raised to second, third, and fourth powers.
- Row 4: **The number 0** is raised to second, third, and fourth powers.

A. 1^2	B. 1^3	C. 1^4
D. 2^2	E. 2^3	F. 2^4
G. $\left(\frac{1}{2}\right)^2$ 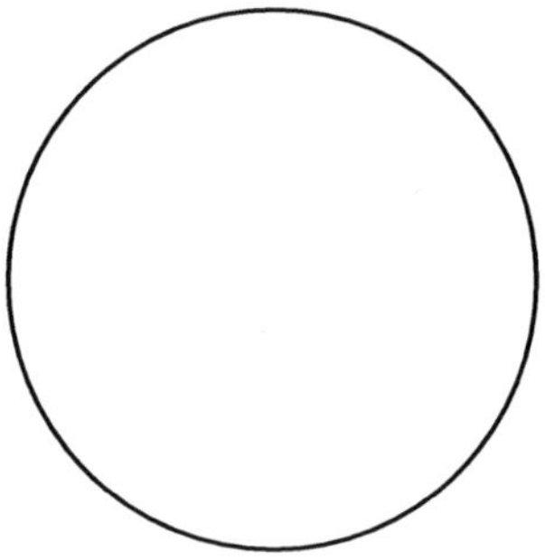	H. $\left(\frac{1}{2}\right)^3$ 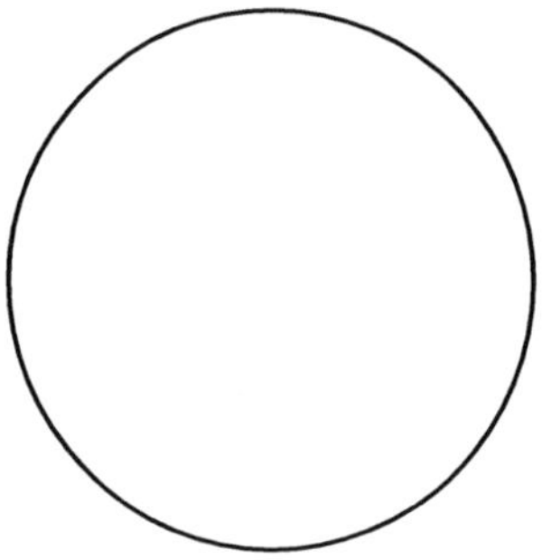	I. $\left(\frac{1}{2}\right)^4$ 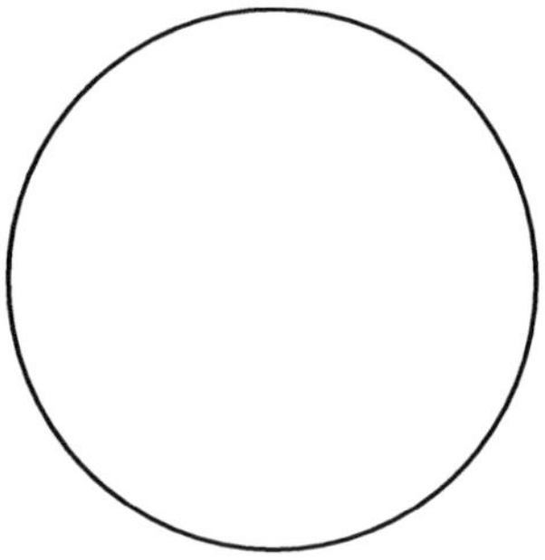
J. 0^2	K. 0^3	L. 0^4

Part 2: Use the symbols greater than (>), less than (<), or equal to (=) to compare by inspection.

M. $\left(\frac{1}{8}\right)^3$ ____ $\left(\frac{1}{8}\right)^2$	N. $\left(\frac{2}{3}\right)^5$ ____ $\left(\frac{2}{3}\right)^2$	O. $\left(\frac{3}{5}\right)^5$ ____ $\left(\frac{3}{5}\right)^9$
P. $\left(\frac{7}{9}\right)^6$ ____ $\left(\frac{7}{9}\right)^8$	Q. Hint: Simplify the fraction first. $\left(\frac{6}{3}\right)^2$ ____ $\left(\frac{6}{3}\right)^3$	R. Hint: Convert to a mixed number first. $\left(\frac{3}{2}\right)^2$ ____ $\left(\frac{3}{2}\right)^3$

Answer Keys and Correcting Student Work

The answer keys in this section are fully annotated. They not only show the correct answer, but also how to get there. This makes is easier to troubleshoot student errors so that they can correct them.

Provide immediate feedback so that students know how they are doing. Take a look at the sample work below.

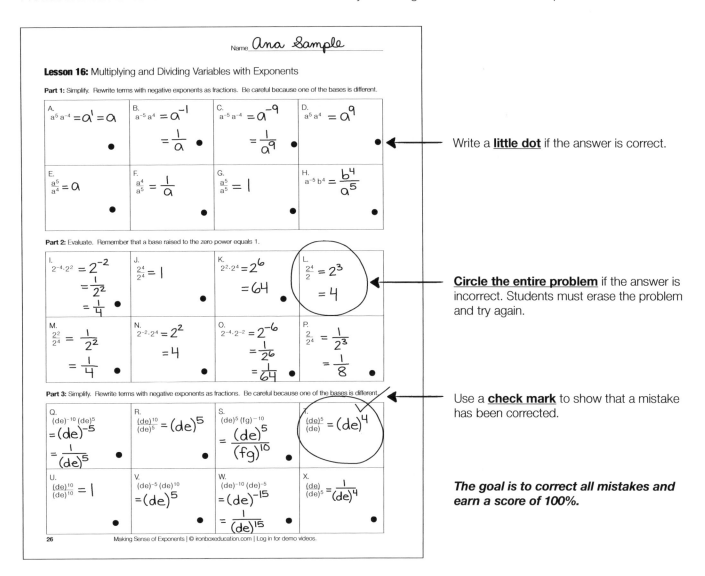

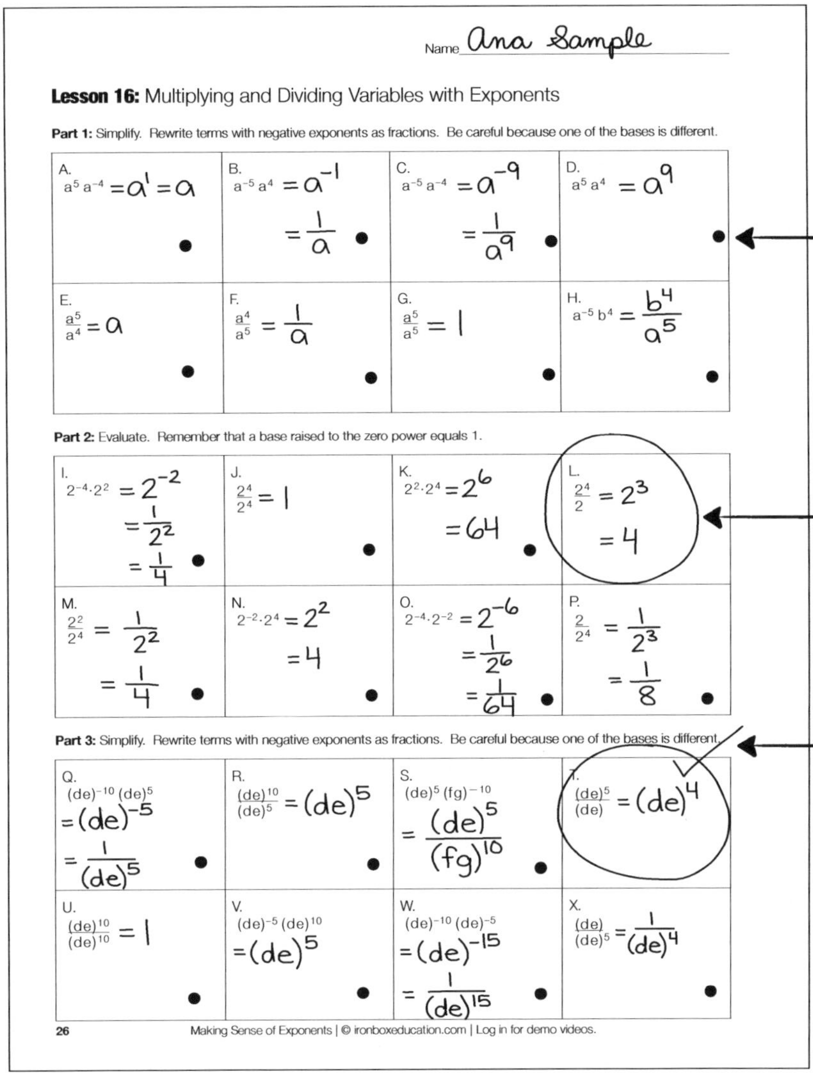

Name Ana Sample

Lesson 16: Multiplying and Dividing Variables with Exponents

Part 1: Simplify. Rewrite terms with negative exponents as fractions. Be careful because one of the bases is different.

A. $a^5 a^{-4} = a^1 = a$ •	B. $a^{-5} a^4 = a^{-1} = \frac{1}{a}$ •	C. $a^{-5} a^{-4} = a^{-9} = \frac{1}{a^9}$ •	D. $a^5 a^4 = a^9$ •
E. $\frac{a^5}{a^4} = a$ •	F. $\frac{a^4}{a^5} = \frac{1}{a}$ •	G. $\frac{a^5}{a^5} = 1$ •	H. $a^{-5} b^4 = \frac{b^4}{a^5}$ •

Part 2: Evaluate. Remember that a base raised to the zero power equals 1.

I. $2^{-4} \cdot 2^2 = 2^{-2} = \frac{1}{2^2} = \frac{1}{4}$ •	J. $\frac{2^4}{2^4} = 1$ •	K. $2^2 \cdot 2^4 = 2^6 = 64$ •	L. $\frac{2^4}{2} = 2^3 = 4$
M. $\frac{2^2}{2^4} = \frac{1}{2^2} = \frac{1}{4}$ •	N. $2^{-2} \cdot 2^4 = 2^2 = 4$ •	O. $2^{-4} \cdot 2^{-2} = 2^{-6} = \frac{1}{2^6} = \frac{1}{64}$ •	P. $\frac{2}{2^4} = \frac{1}{2^3} = \frac{1}{8}$ •

Part 3: Simplify. Rewrite terms with negative exponents as fractions. Be careful because one of the bases is different.

Q. $(de)^{-10} (de)^5 = (de)^{-5} = \frac{1}{(de)^5}$ •	R. $\frac{(de)^{10}}{(de)^5} = (de)^5$ •	S. $(de)^5 (fg)^{-10} = \frac{(de)^5}{(fg)^{10}}$ •	T. $\frac{(de)^5}{(de)} = (de)^4$ ✓
U. $\frac{(de)^{10}}{(de)^{10}} = 1$ •	V. $(de)^{-5} (de)^{10} = (de)^5$ •	W. $(de)^{-10} (de)^{-5} = (de)^{-15} = \frac{1}{(de)^{15}}$ •	X. $\frac{(de)}{(de)^5} = \frac{1}{(de)^4}$ •

26 Making Sense of Exponents | © ironboxeducation.com | Log in for demo videos.

Write a **little dot** if the answer is correct.

Circle the entire problem if the answer is incorrect. Students must erase the problem and try again.

Use a **check mark** to show that a mistake has been corrected.

The goal is to correct all mistakes and earn a score of 100%.

KEY LESSON

Name________________________

Lesson 1: Using Exponents to Show Repeated Multiplication

Use an exponent as a shortcut for writing ***repeated multiplication.***

Example: $2 \times 2 \times 2 \times 2 = 2^4$ base → 2^4 ← exponent "2 to the 4th power"

Part 1: Expand first, then evaluate.

Example: $2^4 = 2 \cdot 2 \cdot 2 \cdot 2$ $= 16$	A. $2^3 = 2 \cdot 2 \cdot 2$ $= 8$	B. $2^5 = 2 \cdot 2 \cdot 2 \cdot 2 \cdot 2$ $= 32$
C. $7^2 = 7 \cdot 7$ $= 49$	D. $8^2 = 8 \cdot 8$ $= 64$	E. $9^2 = 9 \cdot 9$ $= 81$
F. $5^3 = 5 \cdot 5 \cdot 5$ $= 125$	G. $3^4 = (3 \cdot 3)(3 \cdot 3)$ $= 81$	H. $4^4 = 4 \cdot 4 \cdot 4 \cdot 4$ $= 256$
I. $10^2 = 10 \cdot 10$ $= 100$	J. $10^3 = 10 \cdot 10 \cdot 10$ $= 1{,}000$	K. $10^6 = 10 \cdot 10 \cdot 10 \cdot 10 \cdot 10 \cdot 10$ $= 1{,}000{,}000$

Part 2: Expand to show repeated multiplication.

L. $m^3 = m \cdot m \cdot m$	M. $s^2 = s \cdot s$	N. $y^5 = y \cdot y \cdot y \cdot y \cdot y$

Part 3: Simplify using exponents.

O. $12 \times 12 \times 12 \times 12 \times 12$ $= 12^5$	P. $n \cdot n \cdot n \cdot n \cdot n \cdot n \cdot n$ $= n^7$	Q. $x \cdot x \cdot x \cdot x \cdot y \cdot y \cdot y \cdot y \cdot y \cdot z \cdot z$ $= x^4 y^5 z^2$
R. $(n)(n)(n)(n)$ $= n^4$	S. $(x+1)(x+1)(x+1)(x+1)$ $= (x+1)^4$	T. $7(x-3)(x-3)(x-3)(m+5)$ $= 7(x-3)^3(m+5)$

Making Sense of Exponents | © ironboxeducation.com | Log in for demo videos. 11

Key Points from Demo Video – Lesson 1

Using Exponents to Show Repeated Multiplication

Using an exponent is simply a shortcut for repeated multiplication.

In the example, a shorter way of writing 2 x 2 x 2 x 2 is to simply write 2^4. The number 2 is the base. The superscript ^{4} is the exponent, and it shows how many times to multiply the base by itself. The number 2^4 is pronounced, "Two to the fourth power," or, "Two to the fourth."

In Part 1, students expand the expressions to show how exponents represent repeated multiplication. Then, they evaluate each problem.

Part 2 is just like Part 1, but it uses variables as bases instead of numbers as bases.

Part 3 is the reverse of Part 1 and Part 2. Each box shows repeated multiplication, and students need to simplify each expression using exponents.

KEY LESSON

Name________________________

Lesson 2: Graphing Repeated Addition vs. Repeated Multiplication

Directions: Follow along with your instructor to complete this lesson.

Ⓐ Repeated Addition (same addends)			Ⓑ Repeated Multiplication (same factors)		
0 + 0 = 0	4 + 4 = 8	8 + 8 = 16	0 x 0 = 0	4 x 4 = 16	8 x 8 = 64
1 + 1 = 2	5 + 5 = 10	9 + 9 = 18	1 x 1 = 1	5 x 5 = 25	9 x 9 = 81
2 + 2 = 4	6 + 6 = 12	10 + 10 = 20	2 x 2 = 4	6 x 6 = 36	10 x 10 = 100
3 + 3 = 6	7 + 7 = 14		3 x 3 = 9	7 x 7 = 49	

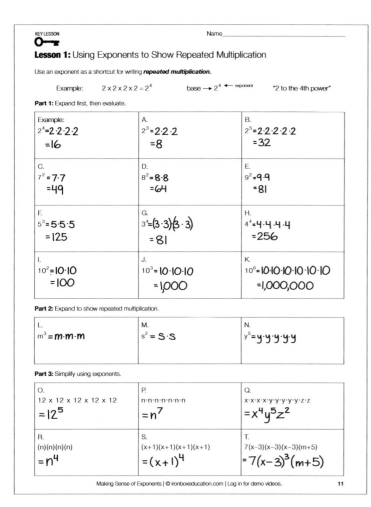

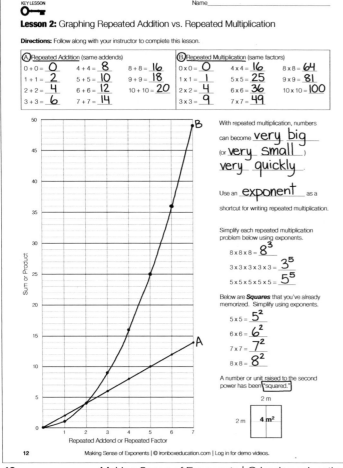

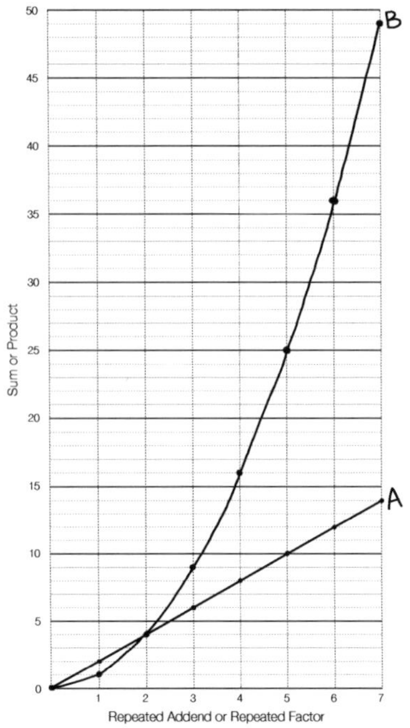

With repeated multiplication, numbers can become very big (or very small) very quickly.

Use an exponent as a shortcut for writing repeated multiplication.

Simplify each repeated multiplication problem below using exponents.

8 x 8 x 8 = 8^3

3 x 3 x 3 x 3 x 3 = 3^5

5 x 5 x 5 x 5 x 5 = 5^5

Below are ***Squares*** that you've already memorized. Simplify using exponents.

5 x 5 = 5^2

6 x 6 = 6^2

7 x 7 = 7^2

8 x 8 = 8^2

A number or unit raised to the second power has been "squared."

2 m

2 m | $4\ m^2$

12 Making Sense of Exponents | © ironboxeducation.com | Log in for demo videos.

Key Points from Demo Video – Lesson 2

Graphing Repeated Addition vs. Repeated Multiplication

Complete Lesson 2 with students to graphically show them the difference between repeated addition and repeated multiplication.

Box A shows repeated addition (the addends are the same). Box B shows repeated multiplication (the factors are the same). Graph the first seven values for repeated addition and for repeated multiplication, as shown in the demo video.

When repeated multiplication is used, numbers can become very big (or very small) very quickly, as shown in the graph.

In the book *10 Powerful Steps to Multiplication Fluency,* students memorized the Squares, such as 5 x 5. Since the Squares show repeated multiplication, they can be written using exponents. For example, 5 x 5 can be written as 5^2.

The diagram on the bottom right of the page shows that when a number or unit is raised to the second power, it has been ***"squared."*** A number such as 2^2 can be pronounced as "2 to the second power" or "2 squared."

KEY LESSON

Name______________________________

Lesson 3: Exponents (1, 10 (Base Ten), Fractions, and Integers as Bases)

Part 1: Follow along with your instructor. Expand each exponent to show repeated multiplication, then evaluate.

A. $3^2 = 3\cdot3$ $= 9$	B. $3^3 = 3\cdot3\cdot3$ $= 27$	C. Use parentheses to help you. $3^4 = (3\cdot3)(3\cdot3)$ $= 81$
D. $1^2 = 1\cdot1$ $= 1$	E. $1^3 = 1\cdot1\cdot1$ $= 1$	F. $1^4 = 1\cdot1\cdot1\cdot1$ $= 1$
G. $10^2 = 10\cdot10$ $= 100$	H. $10^3 = 10\cdot10\cdot10$ $= 1{,}000$	I. $10^4 = 10\cdot10\cdot10\cdot10$ $= 10{,}000$

Part 2: Follow along with your instructor. Expand, evaluate, then shade in the correct fraction of each circle.

J. $(\frac{1}{2})^2 = \frac{1}{2}\cdot\frac{1}{2} = \frac{1}{4}$

K. $(\frac{1}{2})^3 = \frac{1}{2}\cdot\frac{1}{2}\cdot\frac{1}{2} = \frac{1}{8}$

L. $(\frac{1}{2})^4 = \frac{1}{2}\cdot\frac{1}{2}\cdot\frac{1}{2}\cdot\frac{1}{2} = \frac{1}{16}$

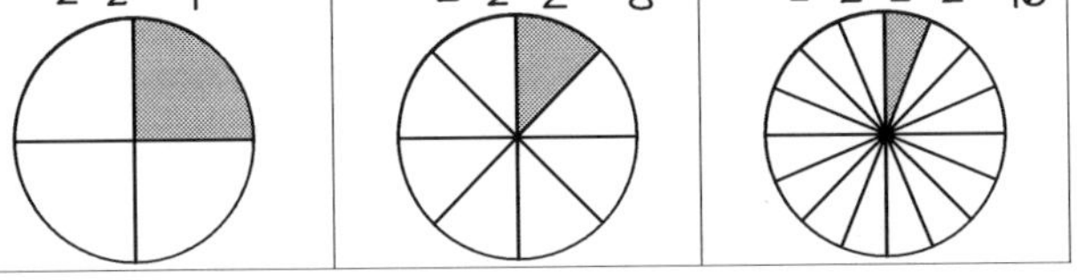

Part 3: Expand, then evaluate. In problems P, Q, R, S, T, and U, write whether your answer is ***positive*** or ***negative.***

M. $(\frac{2}{3})^2$ $= \frac{2}{3}\cdot\frac{2}{3} = \frac{4}{9}$	N. $(\frac{2}{3})^3$ $= \frac{2}{3}\cdot\frac{2}{3}\cdot\frac{2}{3} = \frac{8}{27}$	O. $(\frac{2}{3})^4$ $= \frac{2}{3}\cdot\frac{2}{3}\cdot\frac{2}{3}\cdot\frac{2}{3} = \frac{16}{81}$
P. "negative three" squared $(-3)^2 = (-3)(-3)$ $= 9$ positive	Q. $(-3)^3 = (-3)(-3)(-3)$ $= -27$ negative	R. $(-3)^4 = (-3)(-3)(-3)(-3)$ $= 81$ positive
S. negative "three squared" $-3^2 = -(3\cdot3)$ $= -9$ negative	T. $-3^3 = -(3\cdot3\cdot3)$ $= -27$ negative	U. $-3^4 = -(3\cdot3\cdot3\cdot3)$ $= -81$ negative

Making Sense of Exponents | © ironboxeducation.com | Log in for demo videos. 13

Key Points from Demo Video – Lesson 3

Exponents (1, 10, Fractions, and Integers as Bases)

In Lesson 3, students learn what happens when exponents involve the number 1, the number 10, fractions, and integers as bases.

Problems A, B, and C use the number 3 as a base. As shown in the previous lesson, values can become very big very quickly.

Problems D, E, and F use the number 1 as a base. No matter what exponent is used, the value remains unchanged and is always 1.

Problems G, H, and I use 10 as a base. This is where we get the place value names in the ***base ten*** system, which is also known as the decimal system.

Problems J, K, and L use a fraction as a base. The values get progressively smaller, as shown by shading in the fraction circle.

Problems P, Q, and R use a negative value as a base. Students should pay close attention to the integer rules when completing these problems. This set of problems show that when using exponents with negative numbers as bases, you can end up with positive or negative values.

KEY LESSON

Name______________________________

Lesson 4: Exponential Growth

Directions: Follow along with your instructor to solve the following word problems.

A. Bacterial Growth

At 8:00 a.m., there was a single bacterium on a petri dish. A scientist noticed that the number of bacteria grew exponentially, ***doubling*** every hour. How many bacteria cells will there be at each of the times shown below?

8:00 a.m. 9:00 a.m. 10:00 a.m. 11:00 a.m. 12:00 p.m.

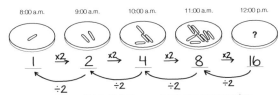

1 →×2→ 2 →×2→ 4 →×2→ 8 →×2→ 16

÷2 ÷2 ÷2 ÷2

- Use arrows to show how to ***multiply by 2*** to find how many bacteria cells there were each hour.
- Use arrows to show how to ***divide by 2*** to find how many bacteria cells there were in the previous hour.

B. Viral Videos

The number of people who viewed a video online grew exponentially. On Sunday, one person viewed the video. Each day after that, ***four times*** as many people viewed the video compared to the day before. Complete the chart to show many people viewed the video each day of the first week. Complete the entire column titled *"Base and Exponent"* first. Note: Lesson 12 (Dividing Variables with Exponents) will further explain why $4^0 = 1$.

Day	Base and Exponent	Views
Sunday	4^0	1
Monday	4^1	4
Tuesday	4^2	16
Wednesday	4^3	64
Thursday	4^4	256
Friday	4^5	1,024
Saturday	4^6	4,096

(×4 arrows down the Views column; ÷4 arrows up the Views column)

Workspace: $16 \times 4 = 64$; $64 \times 4 = 256$; $256 \times 4 = 1{,}024$; $1{,}024 \times 4 = 4{,}096$

- Use arrows to show how to ***multiply by 4*** to find how many views there were each day.
- Use arrows to show how to ***divide by 4*** to find how many views there were the previous day.

14 Making Sense of Exponents | © ironboxeducation.com | Log in for demo videos.

Key Points from Demo Video – Lesson 4

Exponential Growth

Lesson 4 gives students two related examples of exponential growth. Problem A shows bacterial growth, and Problem B uses viral videos.

In problem A, the number of bacteria cells grows exponentially, doubling every hour. Multiply the previous cell count by 2 to find number of bacteria cells in the next hour.

As shown in the answer key, students also draw arrows to show how to multiply by 2 to find out how many bacteria cells there were each hour. Then, they draw arrows showing how to divide by 2 to find how many bacteria cells there were in the previous hour.

Problem A uses the example of a video going "viral" on the internet. The number of views grows exponentially, quadrupling every day. Multiply the previous day's views by 4 to find the number of views the next day.

As in the Problem A, use arrows to show how to multiply by 4 to get the next day's value and how to divide by 4 to get the previous day's value.

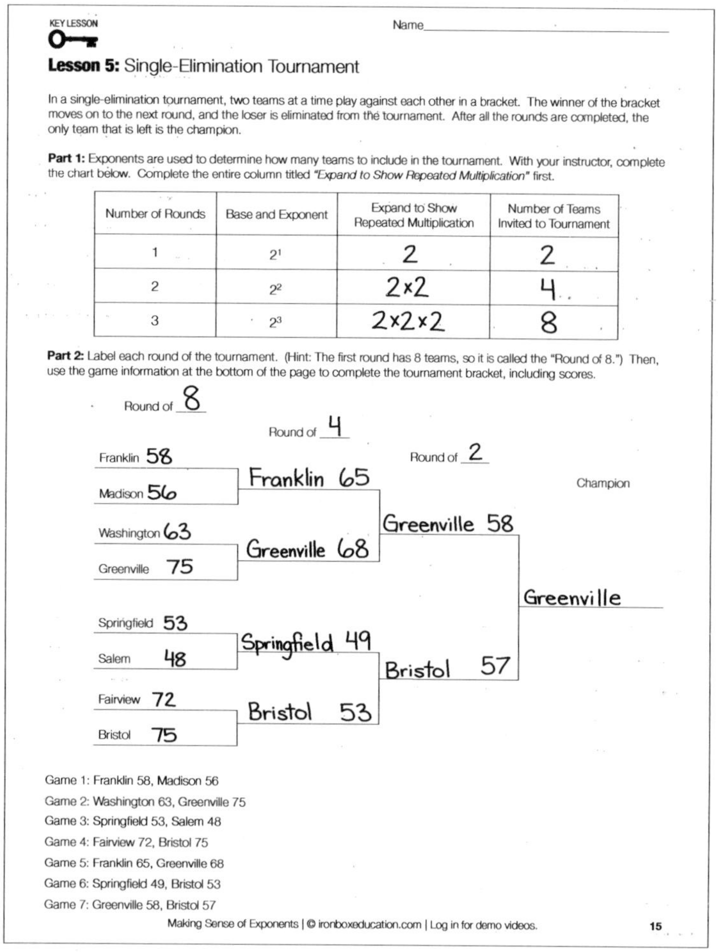
KEY LESSON

Name________________

Lesson 5: Single-Elimination Tournament

In a single-elimination tournament, two teams at a time play against each other in a bracket. The winner of the bracket moves on to the next round, and the loser is eliminated from the tournament. After all the rounds are completed, the only team that is left is the champion.

Part 1: Exponents are used to determine how many teams to include in the tournament. With your instructor, complete the chart below. Complete the entire column titled *"Expand to Show Repeated Multiplication"* first.

Number of Rounds	Base and Exponent	Expand to Show Repeated Multiplication	Number of Teams Invited to Tournament
1	2^1	2	2
2	2^2	2×2	4
3	2^3	2×2×2	8

Part 2: Label each round of the tournament. (Hint: The first round has 8 teams, so it is called the "Round of 8.") Then, use the game information at the bottom of the page to complete the tournament bracket, including scores.

Round of 8 — Round of 4 — Round of 2 — Champion

Franklin 58
Madison 56
Washington 63
Greenville 75
Springfield 53
Salem 48
Fairview 72
Bristol 75

Franklin 65
Greenville 68
Springfield 49
Bristol 53

Greenville 58
Bristol 57

Greenville

Game 1: Franklin 58, Madison 56
Game 2: Washington 63, Greenville 75
Game 3: Springfield 53, Salem 48
Game 4: Fairview 72, Bristol 75
Game 5: Franklin 65, Greenville 68
Game 6: Springfield 49, Bristol 53
Game 7: Greenville 58, Bristol 57

Making Sense of Exponents | © ironboxeducation.com | Log in for demo videos. 15

Key Points from Demo Video – Lesson 5

Single-Elimination Tournament

Lesson 5 shows how exponents are used to determine how many teams to invite to a single-elimination tournament.

In a single-elimination tournament, two teams play against each other in a bracket. The winner of the bracket moves on to the next round, and the loser is eliminated from the tournament. After all the rounds have been completed, the only team that is left is the champion.

In Part 1, complete the chart with students to find out how many teams to invite to a three-round single elimination tournament. Complete the entire column titled *"Expand to Show Repeated Multiplication"* first.

Notice on the chart that 2^1 (2 to the first power) written as repeated multiplication is just 2, so it won't look like repeated multiplication. It will be more obvious to students when they see that 2^2 is 2 x 2 and 2^3 is 2 x 2 x 2.

In Part 2, label the names of the rounds (Round of 8, etc.), then use the game information at the bottom of the page to complete the tournament bracket, including scores. Greenville wins the tournament.

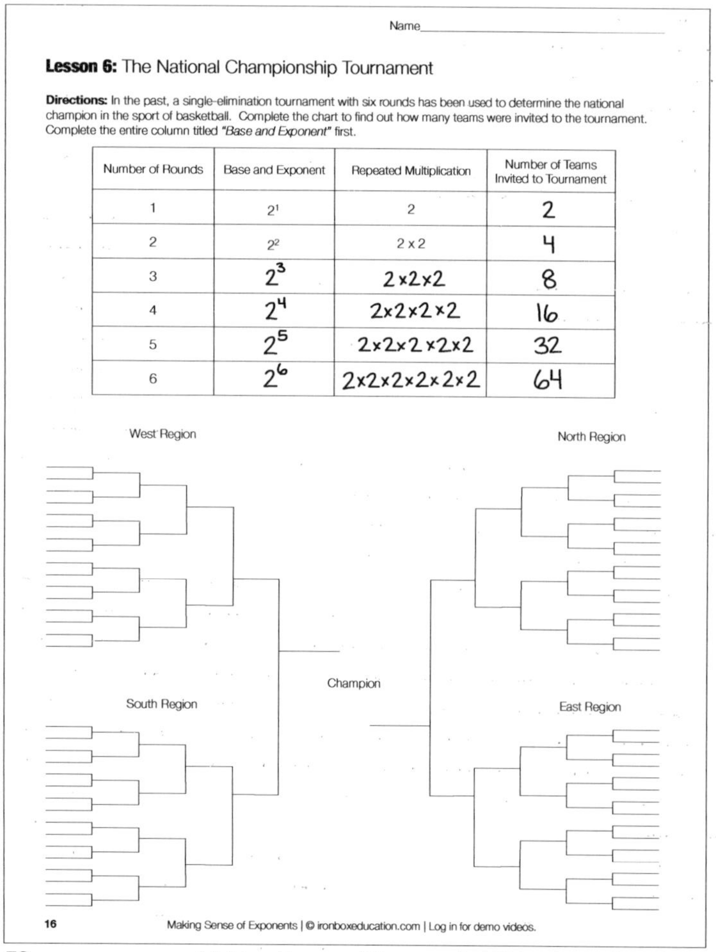
Name________________

Lesson 6: The National Championship Tournament

Directions: In the past, a single-elimination tournament with six rounds has been used to determine the national champion in the sport of basketball. Complete the chart to find out how many teams were invited to the tournament. Complete the entire column titled *"Base and Exponent"* first.

Number of Rounds	Base and Exponent	Repeated Multiplication	Number of Teams Invited to Tournament
1	2^1	2	2
2	2^2	2 x 2	4
3	2^3	2×2×2	8
4	2^4	2×2×2×2	16
5	2^5	2×2×2×2×2	32
6	2^6	2×2×2×2×2×2	64

West Region — North Region — Champion — South Region — East Region

16 Making Sense of Exponents | © ironboxeducation.com | Log in for demo videos.

Key Points from Demo Video – Lesson 6

The National Championship Tournament

In the previous lesson, students used exponents, and they worked with a three-round single-elimination tournament with 8 teams ($2^3 = 8$).

In this lesson, students must find out how many teams get invited to a six-round single-elimination tournament ($2^6 = 64$).

In the past, a six-round single-elimination tournament has been used to determine the national champion in the sport of basketball.

Complete the chart with students. Start by completing the entire column titled *"Base and Exponent"* first.

This lesson shows that a six-round single-elimination tournament includes 64 teams ($2^6 = 64$).

KEY LESSON

Name______________________________

Lesson 7: Adding and Subtracting Variables with Exponents

You learned earlier that you can only add and subtract fractions if they have the same name (denominator). Likewise, you can only ***add*** and ***subtract*** variables with exponents if *they* have the same name (base and exponent) as well.

Part 1: Follow along with your instructor to complete this lesson.

A. 1 apple +1 apple 2 apples	B. 5 pencils −2 pencils 3 pencils	C. 1 fifth +2 fifths 3 fifths	D. 1 half +1 third 1 half + 1 third
E. $3xy$ $+2xy$ $5xy$	F. $9x^2$ $-5x^2$ $4x^2$	G. $4m^2n$ $+2m^2n$ $6m^2n$	H. $2mn$ $+3m^2n$ $2mn + 3m^2n$

Part 2: Simplify. Use parentheses to group terms with the same base and exponent together (think "apples plus apples").

I. $x^2 + (2x + 3x) + 6$ $= x^2 + 5x + 6$	J. $x^2 + (4x - 7x) - 28$ $= x^2 - 3x - 28$	K. $x^2 + (3x + 4x) + 12$ $= x^2 + 7x + 12$	L. $x^2 + (8x + 2x) + 16$ $= x^2 + 10x + 16$
M. $y^2 + (5y + 6y) + 30$ $= y^2 + 11y + 30$	N. $y^2 + (9y - 3y) - 27$ $= y^2 + 6y - 27$	O. $y^2 + (6y + 4y) + 24$ $= y^2 + 10y + 24$	P. $y^2 + (7y + 2y) + 14$ $= y^2 + 9y + 14$

Q. $a^3 + (2a^2 + 4a^2) + (2a + 3a) + 6$ $= a^3 + 6a^2 + 5a + 6$	R. $4a^3 + (1a^2 + 1a^2) + (2a + 3a) + 8$ $= 4a^3 + 2a^2 + 5a + 8$ Careful! Hidden coefficients!
S. $(b^3 + 2b^3) + (2b^2 + 8b^2) + (b + 3b) + 14$ $= 3b^3 + 10b^2 + 4b + 14$	T. $(b^3 + b^3) + (b^2 + b^2) + (b + 3b) + 21$ $= 2b^3 + 2b^2 + 4b + 21$

Making Sense of Exponents | © ironboxeducation.com | Log in for demo videos. 17

Key Points from Demo Video – Lesson 7

Adding and Subtracting Variables with Exponents

In the book *Making Sense of Fractions,* students learned that they can only add and subtract fractions if they have the same "name" (same denominator).

That same concept applies when adding and subtracting variables with exponents. You can only add or subtract variables with exponents if they have the same name (base and exponent) as well.

As shown in the demo video, Part 1 reviews Lesson 7 from the book *Making Sense of Fractions* (The "Same Name" Lesson). It reminds students that it only makes sense to add things together if they have the same name (such as "apples plus apples").

This same concept applies when adding or subtracting fractions (they must have the same denominator) and variables with exponents (they must have the same base and exponent).

In Part 2, students simplify each expression. They should use parentheses to group terms with the same base and exponent together (think "apples plus apples"). Problems R, S, and T have hidden coefficients. The term "a^2" can be written as "$1a^2$," just like an "apple" can be written as "1 apple."

Name______________________________

Lesson 8: Adding and Subtracting Variables with Exponents

You learned earlier that you can only add and subtract fractions if they have the same name (denominator). Likewise, you can only ***add*** and ***subtract*** variables with exponents if *they* have the same name (base and exponent) as well.

Part 1: Follow along with your instructor to complete this lesson.

A. $x^2 + (2x + 3x) + 6$ $= x^2 + 5x + 6$	B. $x^2 + (4x - 5x) - 20$ $= x^2 - 1x - 20$ $= x^2 - x - 20$ Rewrite "−1x" as just "−x."	C. $n^2 + (4n + 3n) + 12$ $= n^2 + 7n + 12$	D. $n^2 + (6n + 7n) + 42$ $= n^2 + 13n + 42$
E. $y^2 + (8y - 8y) - 64$ $= y^2 - 0y - 64$ $= y^2 - 64$ Omit "−0y" from your answer.	F. $y^2 + (7y + 8y) + 56$ $= y^2 + 15y + 56$	G. $a^2 + (5a + 6a) + 30$ $= a^2 + 11a + 30$	H. $a^2 + (5a - 3a) - 15$ $= a^2 - 2a - 15$

Part 2: Simplify. Use parentheses to group terms with the same base and exponent together (think "apples plus apples").

I. $n^3 + (4n^2 + n^2) + (2n + n) + 6$ $= n^3 + 5n^2 + 3n + 6$ Careful! Hidden coefficients!	J. $(4n^3 + n^3) + (n^2 + n^2) + 3n + 8$ $= 5n^3 + 2n^2 + 3n + 8$
K. $(z^3 + z^3) + 2z^2 + (8z + z + 3z) + 4$ $= 2z^3 + 2z^2 + 12z + 4$	L. $(z^3 + 2z^3) + (z^2 + 2z^2) + (3z + z) + 4$ $= 3z^3 + 3z^2 + 4z + 4$
M. $(a^3 + a^3 + a^3) + (a^2 + 4a^2) + a + 8$ $= 3a^3 + 5a^2 + a + 8$	N. $(5a^3 + a^3) + (4a^2 + 2a^2) + (a + 3a) + 26$ $= 6a^3 + 6a^2 + 4a + 26$
O. $(b^4 + b^4) + (b^3 + b^3) + (2b + b) + 6$ $= 2b^4 + 2b^3 + 3b + 6$	P. $(b^4 + 3b^4) + (2b^3 + b^3) + (b^2 + b^2) + b + 14$ $= 4b^4 + 3b^3 + 2b^2 + b + 14$

18 Making Sense of Exponents | © ironboxeducation.com | Log in for demo videos.

Key Points from Demo Video – Lesson 8

Adding and Subtracting Variables with Exponents

Lesson 8 provides students with practice adding and subtracting variables with exponents.

As they learned in the previous lesson, they can only add or subtract variables with exponents if they have the same name (base and exponent). They should use parentheses to group terms with the same base and exponent together (think "apples plus apples").

In Box B, $x^2 - 1x - 20$ can be written as $x^2 - x - 20$.

In Box E, $y^2 - 0y - 64$ can be written as $y^2 - 64$.

Throughout the lesson, there are hidden coefficients. For example, "n^2" can be written as "$1n^2$," just like an "apple" can be written as "1 apple."

KEY LESSON

Name________________

Lesson 9: Multiplying Binomials

Monomial: A single term such as 5xy that involves only one name. The Latin root "nom" means "name."
Think: The term "5 apples" involves only the single name of "apples".

Polynomial: An expression with more than one term summed such as ($5xy + 3x^2y$) that involves more than one name.
Think: The summed expression (5 apples + 3 bananas) involves two names — "apples" and "bananas."

Binomial: A polynomial with exactly two terms summed such as ($5xy + 3x^2y$) that involves two names.
Think: A bicycle has two wheels. A binomial has two terms.

Part 1: Follow along with your instructor to complete this lesson.

A. Standard Algorithm

$$\begin{array}{r} 23 \\ \times\ 22 \\ \hline 146 \\ +460 \\ \hline 506 \end{array}$$

B. Solve the problem to the left by using an expanded approach. Expand 23 into (20 + 3), expand 22 into (20 + 2), then multiply using the same order as the standard algorithm.

$$\begin{array}{r} (20+3) \\ \times\ (20+2) \\ \hline 40+6 \\ 400+60 \\ \hline 400+100+6 = 506 \end{array}$$

C. Expanded Notation

23	
x 22	
6	2 x 3
40	2 x 20
60	20 x 3
+400	20 x 20
506	Sum

D. Solve the problem to the left by drawing an area model.

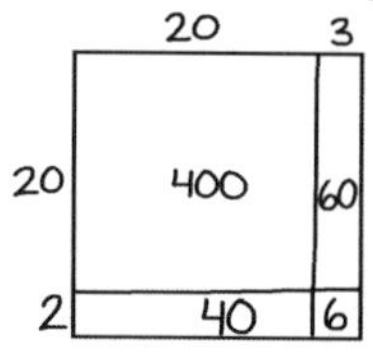

$$\begin{array}{r} 400 \\ 60 \\ 40 \\ +6 \\ \hline 506 \end{array}$$

Part 2: Multiply the binomials. All products will be polynomials and will have an exponent.

E. $$\begin{array}{r} (n+3) \\ \times(n+2) \\ \hline 2n+6 \\ n^2+3n \\ \hline n^2+5n+6 \end{array}$$

F. $$\begin{array}{r} (n+4) \\ \times(n+5) \\ \hline 5n+20 \\ n^2+4n \\ \hline n^2+9n+20 \end{array}$$

G. $$\begin{array}{r} (n+4) \\ \times(n+3) \\ \hline 3n+12 \\ n^2+4n \\ \hline n^2+7n+12 \end{array}$$

Making Sense of Exponents | © ironboxeducation.com | Log in for demo videos. 19

Key Points from Demo Video – Lesson 9

Multiplying Binomials

Multiplying binomials sounds new and complicated, but students will realize that multiplying binomials with two terms is exactly like multiplying numbers with two digits (which is something they have already known how to do for a long time).

Go over the definitions and examples of monomial, polynomial, and binomial at the top of the page. All three words have the Latin root "nom," which means "name." Monomial, polynomial, and binomial simply mean "one name," "many names," and "two names."

- The expression (5 apples + 3 bananas) has two terms and involves two names – apples and bananas.
- The expression ($5xy$ and $3x^2y$) also has two terms and involves two names: xy and x^2y.

In Part 1, Box A shows the standard algorithm for multiplying two-digit numbers. Box B solves the same two-digit multiplication problem using an expanded approach, and it uses the same order of calculations as the standard algorithm.

This same approach is then used in Box B to multiply binomials with two terms, as shown in Part 2.

Name________________

Lesson 10: Multiplying Binomials

Directions: Multiply.

Big Bad Numbers

6 x 6 = 36	7 x 7 = 49	8 x 8 = 64	9 x 9 = 81
6 x 7 = 42	7 x 8 = 56	8 x 9 = 72	
6 x 8 = 48	7 x 9 = 63		
6 x 9 = 54			

Magic Triangle

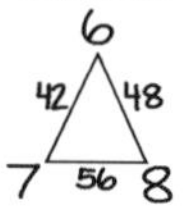

A. $$\begin{array}{r} (n+6) \\ \times(n+8) \\ \hline 8n+48 \\ n^2+6n \\ \hline n^2+14n+48 \end{array}$$

B. $$\begin{array}{r} (n+6) \\ \times(n+7) \\ \hline 7n+42 \\ n^2+6n \\ \hline n^2+13n+42 \end{array}$$

C. $$\begin{array}{r} (n+6) \\ \times(n+5) \\ \hline 5n+30 \\ n^2+6n \\ \hline n^2+11n+30 \end{array}$$

D. $$\begin{array}{r} (n+6) \\ \times(n-9) \\ \hline -9n-54 \\ n^2+6n \\ \hline n^2-3n-54 \end{array}$$

E. $$\begin{array}{r} (n-7) \\ \times(n-7) \\ \hline -7n+49 \\ n^2-7n \\ \hline n^2-14n+49 \end{array}$$

F. $$\begin{array}{r} (n+8) \\ \times(n-8) \\ \hline -8n-64 \\ n^2+8n \\ \hline n^2+0n-64 \\ =n^2-64 \end{array}$$

G. Rewrite vertically, then multiply. $(a+7)(a+9)$

$$\begin{array}{r} (a+7) \\ \times(a+9) \\ \hline 9a+63 \\ a^2+7a \\ \hline a^2+16a+63 \end{array}$$

H. $(a+8)(a+8)$

$$\begin{array}{r} (a+8) \\ \times(a+8) \\ \hline 8a+64 \\ a^2+8a \\ \hline a^2+16a+64 \end{array}$$

I. $(a+8)(a+9)$

$$\begin{array}{r} (a+8) \\ \times(a+9) \\ \hline 9a+72 \\ a^2+8a \\ \hline a^2+17a+72 \end{array}$$

J. $(b+9)(b-7)$

$$\begin{array}{r} (b+9) \\ \times(b-7) \\ \hline -7b-63 \\ b^2+9b \\ \hline b^2+2b-63 \end{array}$$

K. $(b+6)(b-6)$

$$\begin{array}{r} (b+6) \\ \times(b-6) \\ \hline -6b-36 \\ b^2+6b \\ \hline b^2+0b-36 \\ =b^2-36 \end{array}$$

L. $(b+5)(b+5)$

$$\begin{array}{r} (b+5) \\ +(b+5) \\ \hline 5b+25 \\ b^2+5b \\ \hline b^2+10b+25 \end{array}$$

20 Making Sense of Exponents | © ironboxeducation.com | Log in for demo videos.

Key Points from Demo Video – Lesson 10

Multiplying Binomials

In the previous lesson, students saw the strong connection between multiplying binomials and multiplying two-digit numbers with the standard algorithm. Lesson 10 provides them with practice to build their fluency.

In particular, students do the following:

- They work with repeated multiplication of variables, and they write them using exponents. For example, $n \cdot n = n^2$.
- They build the intuition that you can only add or subtract variables with exponents if they have the same name (base and exponent). For example, you can add 8n and 6n together to get 14n because they have the same name (base and exponent).

This set of problems uses the "Big Bad Numbers" and the "Magic Triangle," which students learned in the book *10 Powerful Steps to Multiplication Fluency.*

KEY LESSON

Name________________

Lesson 11: Multiplying Variables with Exponents

Part 1: Expand.

A. $y^3 = y \cdot y \cdot y$	B. $y^4 = y \cdot y \cdot y \cdot y$	C. $x^4 = x \cdot x \cdot x \cdot x$	D. $x^5 = x \cdot x \cdot x \cdot x \cdot x$

Part 2: Expand, multiply, and simplify. Then, look for the shortcut.

E. $a^3 \cdot a^3$ $= a \cdot a \cdot a \cdot a \cdot a \cdot a$ $= a^6$	F. $b^2 \cdot b^3$ $= b \cdot b \cdot b \cdot b \cdot b$ $= b^5$	G. $c^5 \cdot c$ $= c \cdot c \cdot c \cdot c \cdot c \cdot c$ $= c^6$ Careful! Hidden exponent!	H. $d \cdot d^3$ $= d \cdot d \cdot d \cdot d$ $= d^4$

Part 3: Simplify without expanding.

I. $j^4 \cdot j^5 = j^9$	J. $d^7 \cdot d^3 = d^{10}$	K. $e^5 \cdot e = e^6$	L. $x^2 \cdot y^3 = x^2y^3$ Careful! Different bases!
M. $x \cdot x = x^2$	N. $k^4 \cdot m^6 = k^4m^6$	O. $a \cdot a^3 = a^4$	P. $a^3 \cdot a^2 \cdot a = a^6$
Q. $n^4 \cdot n^6 \cdot n^3 = n^{13}$	R. $n^1 \cdot n^2 = n^3$	S. $n^a \cdot n^b = n^{(a+b)}$ The bases are the same, so you can still simplify by adding the exponents (a + b).	T. $n^c \cdot n^d = n^{(c+d)}$

Making Sense of Exponents | © ironboxeducation.com | Log in for demo videos. 21

Key Points from Demo Video – Lesson 11

Multiplying Variables with Exponents

In the previous lessons, students learned to add and subtract variables with exponents. In Lesson 11, they will multiply variables with exponents.

In Part 1, students simply expand each expression to show repeated multiplication.

In Part 2, Box E shows $a^3 \cdot a^3$. Students expand the expression as shown in the answer key. Then, they simplify the product, writing it as a^6.

Students then need to look for the shortcut for multiplying variables with exponents. If the base is the same, keep the base, then add the exponents.

In Part 3, students simplify without expanding first. Be careful with Box L because x^2 and y^3 do not have the same base, so $x^2 \cdot y^3 = x^2y^3$.

Use Box R to help you solve Box S. In both problems, the base is the same, so keep the base, and just add the exponents.

- Box R: $n^1 + n^2 = n^{(1+2)} = n^3$
- Box S: $n^a + n^b = n^{(a+b)}$

KEY LESSON

Name________________

Lesson 12: Dividing Variables with Exponents

Part 1: Expand.

A. $g^3 = g \cdot g \cdot g$	B. $x^4 = x \cdot x \cdot x \cdot x$	C. $m^5 = m \cdot m \cdot m \cdot m \cdot m$	D. $z^6 = z \cdot z \cdot z \cdot z \cdot z \cdot z$

Part 2: Expand, divide, and simplify. Then, look for the shortcut.

E. $\frac{n^5}{n^3} = \frac{n \cdot n \cdot n \cdot n \cdot n}{n \cdot n \cdot n}$ $= n^2$	F. $\frac{x^5}{x^4} = \frac{x \cdot x \cdot x \cdot x \cdot x}{x \cdot x \cdot x \cdot x}$ $= x$	G. $\frac{4^5}{4^3} = \frac{4 \cdot 4 \cdot 4 \cdot 4 \cdot 4}{4 \cdot 4 \cdot 4}$ $= 4^2 = 16$	H. $\frac{4^5}{4^5} = \frac{4 \cdot 4 \cdot 4 \cdot 4 \cdot 4}{4 \cdot 4 \cdot 4 \cdot 4 \cdot 4}$ $= 1$

Part 3: Simplify without expanding. Keep the base, then subtract the exponents.

I. $\frac{a^8}{a^3} = a^5$	J. $\frac{b^5}{b^2} = b^3$	K. $\frac{p^5}{p} = p^4$	L. $\frac{4^5}{4^5} = 4^0 = 1$ Problem H and Problem L show that $4^0 = 1$. A base raised to the zero power equals 1.
M. $\frac{d^5}{e^3} = \frac{d^5}{e^3}$ Already in simplest form. Careful! Different bases!	N. $\frac{5^{100}}{5^{98}} = 5^2 = 25$	O. $\frac{2^9}{2^9} = 2^0 = 1$	P. $\frac{j^{75}}{j^{25}} = j^{50}$
Q. $\frac{k^5m^2}{k^3} = k^2m^2$	R. $\frac{x^5y^4}{y^2} = x^5y^2$	S. $\frac{x^3y^4}{x} = x^2y^4$	T. $\frac{x^6y^3}{x^2y} = x^4y^2$

22 Making Sense of Exponents | © ironboxeducation.com | Log in for demo videos.

Key Points from Demo Video – Lesson 12

Dividing Variables with Exponents

Now that students know how to multiply variables with exponents, Lesson 12 shows them how to divide variables with exponents.

In Part 1, students simply expand each expression to show repeated multiplication.

In Part 2, Box E shows $n^5 \div n^3$. Students expand the problem as shown in the answer key. Then, they simplify the fraction, leaving a quotient of n^2.

Students then need to look for the shortcut for dividing variables with exponents. If the base is the same, keep the base, then subtract the exponents.

In Part 3, students simplify without expanding first. Be careful with Box M because d^5 and e^3 have different bases, so d^5/e^3 is already in simplest form.

Connection to Lesson 4: As shown in the demo video, Box H and Box L show the same problem solved in two different ways. They show why a number raised to the zero power = 1.

Problems Q, R, S, and T involve more than one base. Simply work on one base at a time.

KEY LESSON

Name____________________

Lesson 13: Dividing Variables with Exponents (Negative Exponents)

Part 1: Expand.

A. $h^2 = h \cdot h$	B. $y^5 = y \cdot y \cdot y \cdot y \cdot y$	C. $n^4 = n \cdot n \cdot n \cdot n$	D. $r^2 = r \cdot r$

Part 2: The first row and the second row use the exact same problems, but they will be simplified in two different ways.

- In the ***first row*** (E1, F1, G1, and H1), expand, then simplify each fraction.
- In the ***second row*** (E2, F2, G2, and H2), divide by keeping the base and subtracting the exponents.

E1. Expand, divide, and simplify. $\frac{p^3}{p^5} = \frac{p \cdot p \cdot p}{p \cdot p \cdot p \cdot p \cdot p} = \frac{1}{p^2}$	F1. Expand, divide, and simplify. $\frac{q^3}{q^6} = \frac{q \cdot q \cdot q}{q \cdot q \cdot q \cdot q \cdot q \cdot q} = \frac{1}{q^3}$	G1. Expand, divide, and simplify. $\frac{r^2}{r^5} = \frac{r \cdot r}{r \cdot r \cdot r \cdot r \cdot r} = \frac{1}{r^3}$	H1. Expand, divide, and simplify. $\frac{s^2}{s^6} = \frac{s \cdot s}{s \cdot s \cdot s \cdot s \cdot s \cdot s} = \frac{1}{s^4}$
E2. Subtract the exponents. $\frac{p^3}{p^5} = p^{-2}$	F2. Subtract the exponents. $\frac{q^3}{q^6} = q^{-3}$	G2. Subtract the exponents. $\frac{r^2}{r^5} = r^{-3}$	H2. Subtract the exponents. $\frac{s^2}{s^6} = s^{-4}$

Part 3: Divide by subtracting the exponents. ***For problems Q, R, S, and T, take care of one base at a time.***

I. $\frac{w^7}{w^6} = w^1 = w$	J. $\frac{x^7}{x^2} = x^5$	K. $\frac{y}{y^4} = y^{-3}$	L. $\frac{z^5}{x^3} = \frac{z^5}{x^3}$ Careful! Different bases!
M. $\frac{a^6}{a} = a^5$	N. $\frac{b^{100}}{b^{97}} = b^3$	O. $\frac{c^{11}}{c^{12}} = c^{-1}$	P. $\frac{d^{75}}{d^{100}} = d^{-25}$
Q. $\frac{e^3g^2}{e^4} = e^{-1}g^2$	R. $\frac{h^5j^2}{j^5} = h^5j^{-3}$	S. $\frac{km^4}{k^5} = k^{-4}m^4$	T. $\frac{n^7p}{n^2p^3} = n^5p^{-2}$

Making Sense of Exponents | © ironboxeducation.com | Log in for demo videos. 23

Key Points from Demo Video – Lesson 13

Dividing Variables with Exponents (Negative Exponents)

Lesson 13 is a continuation of Lesson 12 (Dividing Variables with Exponents). The difference is that Lesson 13 involves negative exponents, which will result in fractions.

In Part 1, students expand each expression to show repeated multiplication.

In Part 2, the first row and the second row use the exact same problems, but they are solved in two different ways:

- In the first row, expand first, then simplify each fraction.
- In the second row, divide by keeping the base and subtracting the exponents.

Comparing the results will show how values with negative exponents can be rewritten as fractions.

In Part 3, students divide by keeping the base and subtracting the exponents. In problems Q, R, S, and T, multiple bases are used, so work on one base at a time.

KEY LESSON

Name____________________

Lesson 14: Multiplying Variables with Exponents (Negative Exponents)

Part 1: Add the integers.

A. $5 + -2 = 3$	B. $-5 + 2 = -3$	C. $-5 + -2 = -7$	D. $-5 + -6 = -11$

Part 2: Rewrite using fractions instead of using negative exponents. Refer to Lesson 13, Part 2.

E. $a^{-2} = \frac{1}{a^2}$	F. $b^{-5} = \frac{1}{b^5}$	G. $c^{-4} = \frac{1}{c^4}$	H. $d^{-5} = \frac{1}{d^5}$

Part 3: Simplify. Two of the answers will have negative exponents.

I. $a^5a^{-2} = a^3$	J. $b^7b^{-6} = b^1 = b$	K. $c^4c^{-7} = c^{-3}$	L. $d^{-5}d^{-2} = d^{-7}$

Part 4: Simplify. ***Rewrite terms with negative exponents as fractions.***

M. $w^6w^{-4} = w^2$	N. $w^{-6}w^4 = w^{-2} = \frac{1}{w^2}$	O. $w^{-6}w^{-4} = w^{-10} = \frac{1}{w^{10}}$	P. $w^6c^{-4} = \frac{w^6}{c^4}$ Careful! Different bases!
Q. $x^{-3}x^8 = x^5$	R. $x^{-3}x^{-8} = x^{-11} = \frac{1}{x^{11}}$	S. $x^3m^{-8} = \frac{x^3}{m^8}$	T. $x^3x^{-8} = x^{-5} = \frac{1}{x^5}$
U. $(rst)^{-2}(rst)^{-3} = (rst)^{-5} = \frac{1}{(rst)^5}$	V. $(rst)^2(rst)^3 = (rst)^5$	W. $(rst)^2(rst)^{-3} = (rst)^{-1} = \frac{1}{rst}$	X. $(rst)^{-2}(rst)^3 = rst$

24 Making Sense of Exponents | © ironboxeducation.com | Log in for demo videos.

Key Points from Demo Video – Lesson 14

Multiplying Variables with Exponents (Negative Exponents)

When students worked on multiplying variables with exponents in Lesson 11, all of the exponents were positive. In this lesson, students will multiply variables with negative exponents.

Part 1 is a quick review of adding positive and negative integers, which students will use throughout this lesson.

In Part 2, terms with negative exponents are used. Rewrite them as fractions (see to Lesson 13, Part 2).

In Part 3, multiply by keeping the base and adding the exponents. The product in Problem J is b^1, which can be rewritten as b. Two of the products in Part 3 will have negative exponents.

In Part 4, multiply by keeping the base and adding the exponents. If the product has a negative exponent, rewrite it as a fraction.

Be careful with Problem P because the bases are different.

Name____________________

Lesson 15: Multiplying and Dividing Variables with Exponents

Part 1: Simplify.

A. $x \cdot x = x^2$	B. $j \cdot j^3 = j^4$	C. $d^7 \cdot d = d^8$	D. $k^4 \cdot m^6 = k^4m^6$ Careful! Different bases!
E. $g^{10} \cdot g^{10} = g^{20}$	F. $e^5 \cdot e = e^6$	G. $n^4 \cdot n^3 \cdot n^2 = n^9$	H. $b^2 \cdot b^3 = b^5$
I. $10^4 \cdot 10 = 10^5$ Leave in exponential form.	J. $10^2 \cdot 10^2 \cdot 10^2 = 10^6$ Leave in exponential form.	K. $10^a \cdot 10^b = 10^{(a+b)}$	L. $k^c \cdot m^d = k^cm^d$

Part 2: Simplify.

M. $\frac{j^{10}}{j^4} = j^6$	N. $\frac{c^5}{c} = c^4$	O. $\frac{b^5}{b^2} = b^3$	P. $\frac{d^5}{e^3} = \frac{d^5}{e^3}$ Already in simplest form. Careful! Different bases!
Q. $\frac{10^8}{10^2} = 10^6$ Leave in exponential form.	R. $\frac{10^5}{10} = 10^4$ Leave in exponential form.	S. $\frac{h^9}{x^5} = \frac{h^9}{x^5}$ Already in simplest form.	T. $\frac{3^2}{5^2} = \frac{3^2}{5^2}$ Different bases. Leave in exponential form.
U. $\frac{x^5y^4}{x^2} = x^3y^4$	V. $\frac{x^3y^4}{x} = x^2y^4$	W. $\frac{x^4y^4}{x^2y} = x^2y^3$	X. $\frac{k^5m^2}{k^3m} = k^2m$

Key Points from Demo Video – Lesson 15

Multiplying and Dividing Variables with Exponents

Over the past four lessons, students learned to do the following:

- Multiply variables with exponents by keeping the base and adding the exponents.
- Divide variables with exponents by keeping the base and subtracting the exponents.

Lesson 14 covers both multiplying and dividing variables with exponents.

In Problems D and L, be careful because the bases are different.

Problem K uses non-numerical exponents, but students use the same logic to multiply. Keep the base and add the exponents. $10^a \cdot 10^b = 10^{(a+b)}$.

Problems P and S have different bases and are already in simplest form.

Problem T uses different bases as well (bases of 3 and 5).

In Problems U, V, W, and X, work on one base at a time.

Name____________________

Lesson 16: Multiplying and Dividing Variables with Exponents

Part 1: Simplify. ***Rewrite terms with negative exponents as fractions.*** Be careful of bases that are different.

A. $a^5 a^{-4} = a^1 = a$	B. $a^{-5} a^4 = a^{-1} = \frac{1}{a}$	C. $a^{-5} a^{-4} = a^{-9} = \frac{1}{a^9}$	D. $a^5 a^4 = a^9$
E. $\frac{a^5}{a^4} = a$	F. $\frac{a^4}{a^5} = \frac{1}{a}$	G. $\frac{a^5}{a^5} = 1$	H. $a^{-5} b^4 = \frac{b^4}{a^5}$

Part 2: Evaluate. Remember that a base raised to the zero power equals 1.

I. $2^{-4} \cdot 2^2 = 2^{-2} = \frac{1}{2^2} = \frac{1}{4}$	J. $\frac{2^4}{2^4} = 1$	K. $2^2 \cdot 2^4 = 2^6 = 64$	L. $\frac{2^4}{2} = 2^3 = 8$
M. $\frac{2^2}{2^4} = \frac{1}{2^2} = \frac{1}{4}$	N. $2^{-2} \cdot 2^4 = 2^2 = 4$	O. $2^{-4} \cdot 2^{-2} = 2^{-6} = \frac{1}{2^6} = \frac{1}{64}$	P. $\frac{2}{2^4} = \frac{1}{2^3} = \frac{1}{8}$

Part 3: Simplify. ***Rewrite terms with negative exponents as fractions.*** Be careful of bases that are different.

Q. $(de)^{-10}(de)^5 = (de)^{-5} = \frac{1}{(de)^5}$	R. $\frac{(de)^{10}}{(de)^5} = (de)^5$	S. $(de)^5 (fg)^{-10} = \frac{(de)^5}{(fg)^{10}}$	T. $\frac{(de)^5}{(de)} = (de)^4$
U. $\frac{(de)^{10}}{(de)^{10}} = 1$	V. $(de)^{-5}(de)^{10} = (de)^5$	W. $(de)^{-10}(de)^{-5} = (de)^{-15} = \frac{1}{(de)^{15}}$	X. $\frac{(de)}{(de)^5} = \frac{1}{(de)^4}$

Key Points from Demo Video – Lesson 16

Multiplying and Dividing Variables with Exponents

Lesson 15 reviewed multiplying and dividing variables with fractions, and all the exponents were positive.

Lesson 16 continues the review of multiplying and dividing variables with fractions, and this lesson includes both positive and negative exponents.

If a product or quotient involves a negative exponent, students should rewrite them as fractions.

Part 1 and Part 3 use variables as bases. Part 2 uses a base of 2, and students will evaluate these problems completely. For example, in Problem N, the final answer should be 4 and not just 2^2.

KEY LESSON

Name____________________

Lesson 17: Comparing Numbers with Exponents

Part 1: Evaluate.

A. $2^1 = 2$	B. $5^1 = 5$	C. $24^1 = 24$
D. $2^0 = 1$	E. $5^0 = 1$	F. $37^0 = 1$
G. $1^3 = 1$	H. $1^5 = 1$	I. $1^{100} = 1$
J. Use parentheses to help you. 3^4 $=(3\cdot3)(3\cdot3)$ $=81$	K. 4^5 $=4\cdot4\cdot4\cdot4\cdot4$ $=1{,}024$	L. Use parentheses and Box K to help you. 2^{10} $=(2\cdot2)(2\cdot2)(2\cdot2)(2\cdot2)(2\cdot2)$ $=1{,}024$
M. $(-4)^2 = (-4)(-4)$ $= 16$	N. $-4^2 = -(4\cdot4)$ $= -16$	O. $-(4^2) = -(4\cdot4)$ $= -16$

Part 2: Use the symbols greater than (>), less than (<), or equal to (=) to compare exponents. Use the white space to show your work. Remember that a base raised to the zero power equals 1.

P. $2^3 < 3^2$; $8 < 9$	Q. $2^4 = 4^2$; $16 = 16$	R. $2^5 > 5^2$; $32 > 25$
S. Use Box J to help you. $3^4 > 4^3$; $81 > 64$	T. Use Box L to help you. $2^{10} > 10^2$; $1{,}024 > 100$	U. Use Box L and Box K to help you. $2^{10} = 4^5$; $1{,}024 = 1{,}024$
V. $1^{100} < 100^1$; $1 < 100$	W. $5^0 = 37^0$; $1 = 1$	X. $0^0 = 1^0$; $1 = 1$
Y. $(-4)^2 > -4^2$; $16 > -16$	Z. $-4^2 = -(4^2)$; $-16 = -16$	AA. $-(4^2) < (-4)^2$; $-16 < 16$

Making Sense of Exponents | © ironboxeducation.com | Log in for demo videos. 27

Key Points from Demo Video – Lesson 17

Comparing Numbers with Exponents

In Lesson 17, students compare the magnitudes of numbers with exponents.

Part 1 shows that:

- A number raised to the first power equals the same number.
- A number raised to the zero power equals 1.
- The number 1 raised to any power equals 1.

Use parentheses in Problem G to make it easier to multiply.

$$3^4$$
$$= 3 \cdot 3 \cdot 3 \cdot 3$$
$$= (3 \cdot 3) \cdot (3 \cdot 3)$$
$$= 9 \cdot 9$$
$$= 81$$

Part 2 involves using the symbols greater than (>), less than (<), and equal to (=) to compare numbers with exponents. Students should use the white space in each box to show their work.

KEY LESSON

Name____________________

Lesson 18: Scientific Notation

Part 1: Follow along with your instructor to complete this lesson. Expand and evaluate.

A. $10^2 = 10\cdot10$ $=100$	B. $10^3 = 10\cdot10\cdot10$ $=1{,}000$	C. Evaluate without expanding. 10^6 $=1{,}000{,}000$	D. Evaluate without expanding. 10^5 $=100{,}000$

Part 2: Rewrite these ***powers of ten*** using exponents.

E. 1,000 $=10^3$	F. 100 $=10^2$	G. 100,000 $=10^5$	H. 1,000,000 $=10^6$

Part 3: Factor into a single-digit number times a power of ten. Then, write that power of ten using an exponent.

Example: 700 $=7 \times 100$ $=7\times10^2$	I. 9,000 $=9 \times 1{,}000$ $=9\times10^3$	J. 3,000,000 $=3 \times 1{,}000{,}000$ $=3\times10^6$	K. 6,000,000,000,000 $=6\times10^{12}$ Go straight to the answer without factoring.

Part 4: Circle the number that is not written in normalized scientific notation. Explain why it is not in scientific notation.

L. 8.3×10^3 7.2×10^5 13.4×10^4 3.6×10^7 — 13 is not a single digit between 1–9.	M. 4.2×10^6 1.7×8^3 3.9×10^2 5.6×10^5 — 8^3 is not a power of 10.	N. 3.335×10^8 4.2623×10^3 0.2623×10^9 3.35×10^6 — 0 is not a single digit between 1–9.	O. 4.7×10^{-8} 3.8×10^{-9} 6.5×10^{-5} 12.3×10^{-2} — 12 is not a single digit between 1–9.

Part 5: Write each number in scientific notation without factoring first. Target your new decimal point FIRST.

P. 1,345 $=1.345 \times 10^3$	Q. 3,250,000 $=3.25 \times 10^6$	R. Notice the decimal point! 103,000.00 $=1.03 \times 10^5$	S. Notice the decimal point! 467,300,000.0 $=4.673 \times 10^8$
T. .00023 $=2.3 \times 10^{-4}$	U. .00000594 $=5.94 \times 10^{-6}$	V. 0.0000001 $=1\times10^{-7} = 10^{-7}$	W. 0.00058 $=5.8 \times 10^{-4}$

28 Making Sense of Exponents | © ironboxeducation.com | Log in for demo videos.

Key Points from Demo Video – Lesson 18

Scientific Notation

Lesson 18 is a key lesson in which the instructor helps students use their understanding of exponents to make sense of scientific notation.

In Part 1, students expand and evaluate a base of 10 raised to powers of 2, 3, 6, and 5.

Part 2 is the opposite of Part 1. Powers of 10 are written using exponents.

In Part 3, factor each number into a single-digit number multiplied by a power of 10, as shown in the example. Then, write that power of 10 using exponents. The number is now in scientific notation.

In each problem in Part 4, three out of four numbers are written in scientific notation, and one of them is not. Students circle the number that is not written in normalized scientific notation, and they explain how they can tell that it's not in scientific notation.

In Part 5, students write numbers in scientific notation, as shown in the demo video. The first row involves very large numbers (positive exponents), and the last row involves very small decimals (negative exponents).

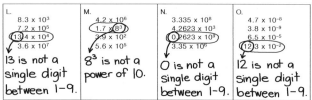

Name____________________

Lesson 19: Scientific Notation

Part 1: Evaluate.

A. 8.3×10^3 $=8{,}300$	B. 7.2×10^5 $=720{,}000$	C. 3.35×10^6 $=3{,}350{,}000$	D. 4.2623×10^3 $=4{,}262.3$
E. 1.23×10^2 $=123$	F. 6.5×10^5 $=650{,}000$	G. 3.8×10^4 $=38{,}000$	H. 4.732×10^2 $=473.2$

Part 2: Write in scientific notation. All of these problems contain negative exponents.

I. 1.23×10^{-2} $=0.0123$	J. 6.5×10^{-5} $=0.000065$	K. 3.8×10^{-4} $=0.00038$	L. 4.732×10^{-2} $=0.04732$

Part 3: Write in scientific notation. Target your new decimal point first.

M. 1,350 $= 1.35 \times 10^3$	N. 1,350,000 $=1.35 \times 10^6$	O. 13,500,000.0 $=1.35 \times 10^7$	P. 135,000,000.0 $=1.35 \times 10^8$
Q. 0.135 $=1.35 \times 10^{-1}$	R. 0.0000135 $=1.35 \times 10^{-5}$	S. 0.0135 $=1.35 \times 10^{-2}$	T. 0.00000000135 $=1.35 \times 10^{-9}$

Part 4: Write in scientific notation. Target your new decimal point first.

U. 275,000 $=2.75 \times 10^5$	V. 4,850,000 $=4.85 \times 10^6$	W. 9,000,000 $=9 \times 10^6$	X. 25,250,000 $=2.525 \times 10^7$
Y. 0.509 $=5.09 \times 10^{-1}$	Z. 0.00509 $=5.09 \times 10^{-3}$	AA. 0.051 $=5.1 \times 10^{-2}$	AB. 0.0000000401 $=4.01 \times 10^{-8}$

Making Sense of Exponents | © ironboxeducation.com | Log in for demo videos. 29

Key Points from Demo Video – Lesson 19

Scientific Notation

In Lesson 19, students practice going back and forth between:

- standard decimal notation (i.e., 650,000)
- scientific notation (i.e., 6.5×10^5)

These problems include very large numbers that use positive exponents and very small decimals that use negative exponents.

To go from standard decimal notation to scientific notation, students should target their new decimal point first. When students target their new decimal point, the whole number to the left of the decimal point should be a single digit between 1 and 9.

Then, they count the number of decimal places (or place values) to the left or right of the old decimal point.

- If they move to the right, the exponent will be positive because on a number line, positive numbers are to the right of zero.
- If they move to the left, the exponent will be negative.

Name____________________

Lesson 20: Exponents Review

Part 1: Add or subtract.

A. $6xy$ $+4xy$ $10xy$	B. $8x^2$ $-3x^2$ $5x^2$	C. $5m^2n$ $-2m^2n$ $3m^2n$	D. $4mn$ $+3m^2n$ $4mn+3m^2n$

Part 2: Simplify. Rewrite terms with negative exponents as fractions. ***Leave problems G and L in exponential form.***

E. $a^6a^{-4} = a^2$	F. $(xyz)^{-6}(xyz)^4$ $=(xyz)^{-2}$ $=\frac{1}{(xyz)^2}$	G. $23^{-6}23^{-4}$ $=23^{-10}$ $=\frac{1}{23^{10}}$	H. $h^6w^{-4} = \frac{h^6}{w^4}$
I. $\frac{b^5}{b^3} = b^2$	J. $\frac{b^3}{b^5} = b^{-2}$ $=\frac{1}{b^2}$	K. $\frac{c^5d^7}{c^5d^3} = d^4$	L. $\frac{15^7 23^6}{15^2 23^8}$ $=15^5 23^{-2}$ $=\frac{15^5}{23^2}$

Part 3: Evaluate.

M. 4.25×10^6 $=4250000$	N. 7.3245×10^3 $=7{,}324.5$	O. 9.8×10^{-4} $=0.00098$	P. 5.632×10^{-2} $=0.05632$

Part 4: Write each number in scientific notation. Target your new decimal point FIRST.

Q. 365,000 $=3.65 \times 10^5$	R. 7,950,000 $=7.95 \times 10^6$	S. 0.00409 $=4.09 \times 10^{-3}$	T. 0.081 $=8.1 \times 10^{-2}$

30 Making Sense of Exponents | © ironboxeducation.com | Log in for demo videos.

Key Points from Demo Video – Lesson 20

Exponents Review

Lesson 20 reviews the following operations involving exponents:

- adding
- subtracting
- multiplying
- dividing

This lesson involves both of the following:

- values with positive exponents
- values with negative exponents, which are to be rewritten as fractions

Finally, students review going back and forth between the following:

- standard decimal notation
- scientific notation

Name____________________

Lesson 21: Exponents Review

Part 1: Add or subtract.

A.	B.	C.	D.
7abc −3abc 4abc	$9y^2$ $+2y^2$ $11y^2$	$4c^2d$ $-3c^2d$ c^2d	$5m^2n$ $+6m^2n$ $11m^2n$

Part 2: Simplify. Rewrite terms with negative exponents as fractions. ***Leave problems G and L in exponential form.***

E. $w^3w^{-8} = w^{-5} = \frac{1}{w^5}$	F. $(abc)^{-4}(abc)^2 = (abc)^{-2} = \frac{1}{(abc)^2}$	G. $3^{-4}3^{-2} = 3^{-6} = \frac{1}{3^6}$	H. $m^6m^{-4} = m^2$
I. $\frac{n^9}{n^7} = n^2$	J. $\frac{n^7}{n^9} = n^{-2} = \frac{1}{n^2}$	K. $\frac{r^5s^3}{r^4s^8} = rs^{-5} = \frac{r}{s^5}$	L. $\frac{25^4 43^6}{25^2 43^9} = 25^2 43^{-3} = \frac{25^2}{43^3}$

Part 3: Evaluate.

M.	N.	O.	P.
6.25×10^5 $= 625{,}000$	8.3445×10^2 $= 834.45$	8.4×10^{-3} $= 0.0084$	3.141×10^{-3} $= 0.003141$

Part 4: Write each number in scientific notation. Target your new decimal point FIRST.

Q.	R.	S.	T.
525,600 $= 5.256 \times 10^5$	5,150,000 $= 5.15 \times 10^6$	0.00405 $= 4.05 \times 10^{-3}$	0.042 $= 4.2 \times 10^{-2}$

Making Sense of Exponents | © ironboxeducation.com | Log in for demo videos. 31

Key Points from Demo Video – Lesson 21

Exponents Review

Lesson 21 reviews the following operations involving exponents:

- adding
- subtracting
- multiplying
- dividing

This lesson involves both of the following:

- values with positive exponents
- values with negative exponents, which are to be rewritten as fractions

Finally, students review going back and forth between the following:

- standard decimal notation
- scientific notation

KEY LESSON

Name____________________

Lesson 22: Diamond Puzzles

Part 1: Factor.

A. 12	B. 16	C. 18	D. 20
1 · 12 2 · 6 3 · 4	1 · 16 2 · 8 4 · 4	1 · 18 2 · 9 3 · 6	1 · 20 2 · 10 4 · 5

Part 2: Solve each puzzle by finding the two numbers whose ***product*** is equal to the number at the top of the diamond and whose ***sum*** is equal to the number at the bottom of the diamond. The solution for the example is 6 and 2 because 6 x 2 = 12 and 6 + 2 = 8.

	Top	Left	Right	Bottom
Ex.	12	6	2	8
E.	16	4	4	8
F.	12	12	1	13
G.	18	18	1	19
H.	18	9	2	11
I.	20	4	5	9
J.	12	3	4	7
K.	16	16	1	17
L.	20	20	1	21
M.	16	8	2	10
N.	18	6	3	9
O.	20	10	2	12

32 Making Sense of Exponents | © ironboxeducation.com | Log in for demo videos.

Key Points from Demo Video – Lesson 22

Diamond Puzzles

The ability to work fluently with values involving exponents (adding, subtracting, multiplying, and dividing) helps students crack the code to higher level math concepts that they will encounter in algebra.

One such algebraic concept is factoring quadratic expressions, which will be covered in the next lesson.

In this lesson, students work with easy-to-solve diamond puzzles that will prepare them for the upcoming assignment.

In Part 1, students write the factors for 12, 16, 18, and 20. These factors will be used in Part 2.

In Part 2, students solve each diamond puzzle by finding the two numbers whose ***product*** is equal to the number at the top of the diamond and whose ***sum*** is equal to the number at the bottom of the diamond.

The solution for the example is 6 and 2 (or 2 and 6) because 6 x 2 = 12 and 6 + 2 = 8.

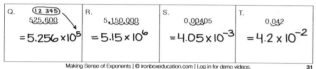

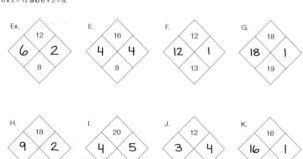

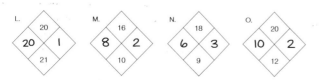

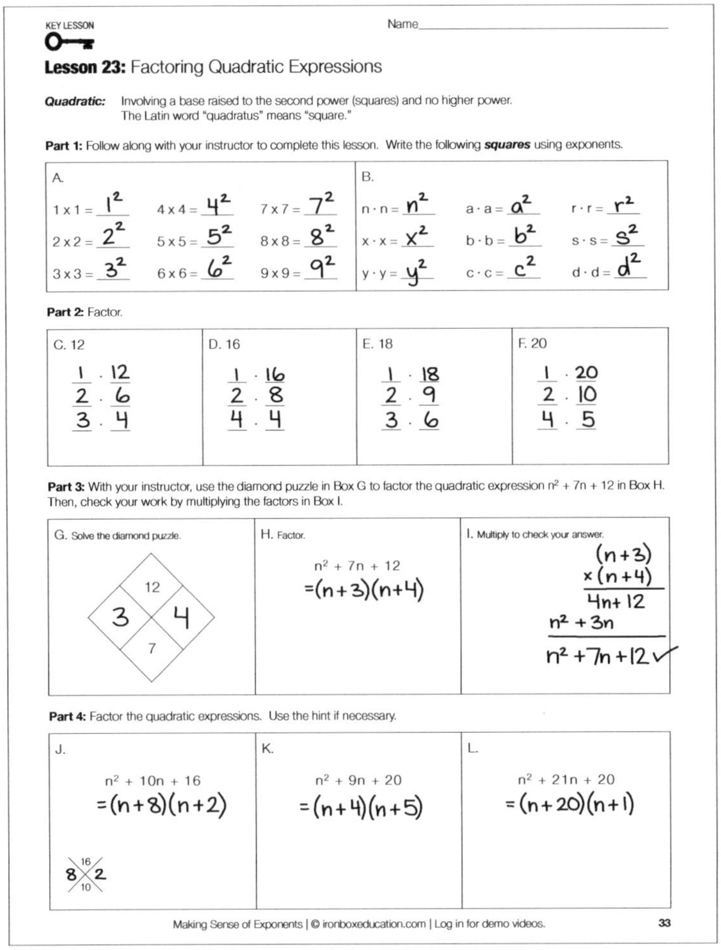

Name_____

Lesson 23: Factoring Quadratic Expressions

Quadratic: Involving a base raised to the second power (squares) and no higher power.
The Latin word "quadratus" means "square."

Part 1: Follow along with your instructor to complete this lesson. Write the following ***squares*** using exponents.

A.

$1 \times 1 = 1^2$	$4 \times 4 = 4^2$	$7 \times 7 = 7^2$
$2 \times 2 = 2^2$	$5 \times 5 = 5^2$	$8 \times 8 = 8^2$
$3 \times 3 = 3^2$	$6 \times 6 = 6^2$	$9 \times 9 = 9^2$

B.

$n \cdot n = n^2$	$a \cdot a = a^2$	$r \cdot r = r^2$
$x \cdot x = x^2$	$b \cdot b = b^2$	$s \cdot s = s^2$
$y \cdot y = y^2$	$c \cdot c = c^2$	$d \cdot d = d^2$

Part 2: Factor.

C. 12	D. 16	E. 18	F. 20
$1 \cdot 12$	$1 \cdot 16$	$1 \cdot 18$	$1 \cdot 20$
$2 \cdot 6$	$2 \cdot 8$	$2 \cdot 9$	$2 \cdot 10$
$3 \cdot 4$	$4 \cdot 4$	$3 \cdot 6$	$4 \cdot 5$

Part 3: With your instructor, use the diamond puzzle in Box G to factor the quadratic expression $n^2 + 7n + 12$ in Box H.
Then, check your work by multiplying the factors in Box I.

G. Solve the diamond puzzle.

(diamond: top 12, left 3, right 4, bottom 7)

H. Factor.

$n^2 + 7n + 12$
$= (n+3)(n+4)$

I. Multiply to check your answer.

$$\begin{array}{r} (n+3) \\ \times (n+4) \\ \hline 4n+12 \\ n^2 + 3n \\ \hline n^2 + 7n + 12 \checkmark \end{array}$$

Part 4: Factor the quadratic expressions. Use the hint if necessary.

J.

$n^2 + 10n + 16$
$= (n+8)(n+2)$

(hint X: 16 top, 8 and 2 sides, 10 bottom)

K.

$n^2 + 9n + 20$
$= (n+4)(n+5)$

L.

$n^2 + 21n + 20$
$= (n+20)(n+1)$

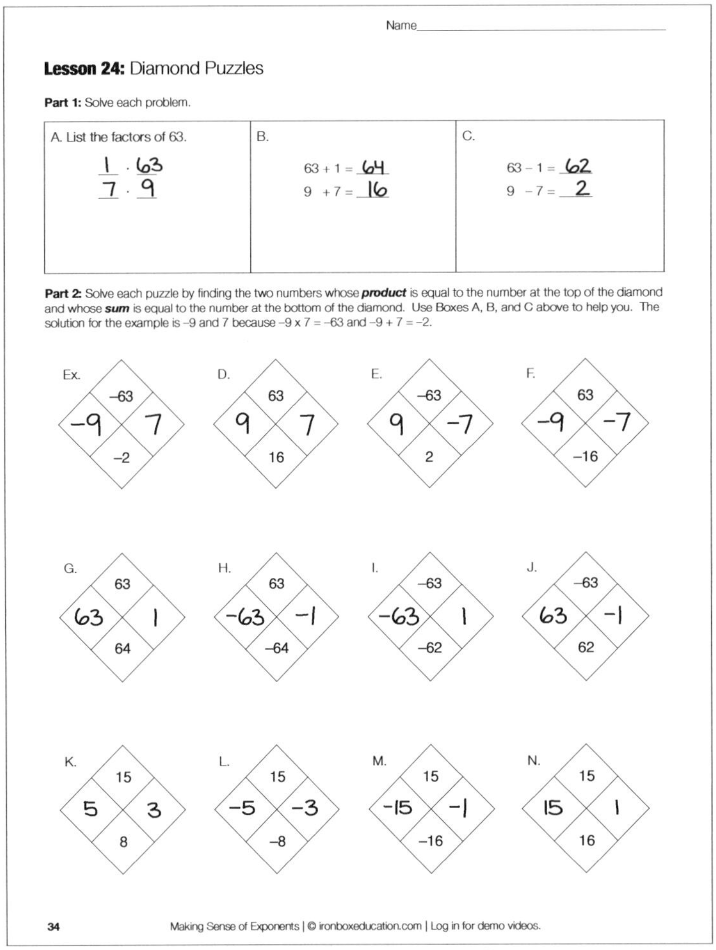

Name_____

Lesson 24: Diamond Puzzles

Part 1: Solve each problem.

A. List the factors of 63.	B.	C.
$1 \cdot 63$	$63 + 1 = 64$	$63 - 1 = 62$
$7 \cdot 9$	$9 + 7 = 16$	$9 - 7 = 2$

Part 2: Solve each puzzle by finding the two numbers whose ***product*** is equal to the number at the top of the diamond and whose ***sum*** is equal to the number at the bottom of the diamond. Use Boxes A, B, and C above to help you. The solution for the example is –9 and 7 because –9 x 7 = –63 and –9 + 7 = –2.

Ex. (top –63, left –9, right 7, bottom –2)

D. (top 63, left 9, right 7, bottom 16)

E. (top –63, left 9, right –7, bottom 2)

F. (top 63, left –9, right –7, bottom –16)

G. (top 63, left 63, right 1, bottom 64)

H. (top 63, left –63, right –1, bottom –64)

I. (top –63, left –63, right 1, bottom –62)

J. (top –63, left 63, right –1, bottom 62)

K. (top 15, left 5, right 3, bottom 8)

L. (top 15, left –5, right –3, bottom –8)

M. (top 15, left –15, right –1, bottom –16)

N. (top 15, left 15, right 1, bottom 16)

Key Points from Demo Video – Lesson 23
Factoring Quadratic Expressions

An expression that is "quadratic" involves a base raised to the second power (squares) and no higher power. The Latin word "quadratus" means "square." This is why in Part 1, students rewrite squares using exponents. For example, 9 squared (9 x 9) is written as 9^2, and n squared (n · n) is written as n^2.

In Part 2, students factor the numbers 12, 16, 18, and 20. These factors will be used in Parts 3 and 4.

In Part 3, students solve the diamond puzzle shown in the answer key. Then, the instructor helps them use this solution to factor the quadratic expression $n^2 + 7n + 12$. Remember, "quadratus" means "square," so this expression is quadratic because it involves a square (n^2 or n "squared").

The factors are (n + 3) and (n + 4). In Box I, students multiply these two factors to check their work. This is just like Lesson 9 (Multiplying Binomials).

In Part 4, students factor quadratic expressions. If necessary, students can use a hint by writing a big "X" and solving a diamond puzzle, as shown in Box J. The constant (value without variables) goes at the top of the diamond.

Key Points from Demo Video – Lesson 24
Diamond Puzzles

In the previous two lessons, students worked with easy-to-solve diamond puzzles to help them factor quadratic expressions.

"Quadratus" means "square" in Latin, so quadratic expressions involve squares (a base raised to the second power and no higher power).

In Lesson 24, students will work with diamond puzzles that are a little more challenging.

In Part 1, students factor the numbers 24, 30, and 36. These numbers are more challenging to work with than the previous two lessons because these numbers have more factors.

In Part 2, students solve diamond puzzles that involve the products of 24, 30, and 36.

Hint: In Problem E, the product is 24, and the sum is 25 (just one higher). This difference of 1 is a telltale sign that the factors will be 24 (same as the product) and the number 1.

In Problem M, the product is 36, and the sum is 37. The factors will be 36 and 1.

Name____________________

Lesson 25: Factoring Quadratic Expressions

Part 1: Factor.

A. List the factors of 63.	B.	C.
1 · 63 7 · 9	63 + 1 = 64 9 + 7 = 16	63 − 1 = 62 9 − 7 = 2

Part 2: Factor the quadratic expressions in ***Row 1.*** Then, use multiplication in ***Row 2*** to check your work.

D1.	E1.	F1.
$x^2 + 64x + 63$ $= (x+63)(x+1)$ (X: 63 top, 63 and 1 sides, 64 bottom)	$x^2 + 16x + 15$ $= (x+15)(x+1)$	$x^2 + 16x + 63$ $= (x+7)(x+9)$
D2. Multiply to check your answer above. $(x+63)$ $\cdot (x+1)$ $x + 63$ $x^2 + 63x$ $x^2 + 64x + 63$ ✓	E2. Multiply to check your answer above. $(x+15)$ $\cdot (x+1)$ $x + 15$ $x^2 + 15x$ $x^2 + 16x + 15$ ✓	F2. Multiply to check your answer above. $(x+7)$ $\cdot (x+9)$ $9x + 63$ $x^2 + 7x$ $x^2 + 16x + 63$ ✓

Part 3: Factor the quadratic expressions in ***Row 1.*** Then, use multiplication in ***Row 2*** to check your work.

G1.	H1.	I1.
$n^2 - 2n - 63$ $(n-9)(n+7)$ (X: −63 top, −9 and 7 sides, −2 bottom)	$n^2 + 2n - 63$ $= (n+9)(n-7)$	$n^2 - 64n + 63$ $= (n-63)(n-1)$
G2. Multiply to check your answer above. $(n-9)$ $\cdot (n+7)$ $7n - 63$ $n^2 - 9n$ $n^2 - 2n - 63$ ✓	H2. Multiply to check your answer above. $(n+9)$ $\cdot (n-7)$ $-7n - 63$ $n^2 + 9n$ $n^2 + 2n - 63$ ✓	I2. Multiply to check your answer above. $(n-63)$ $\cdot (n-1)$ $-n + 63$ $n^2 - 63n$ $n^2 - 64n + 63$ ✓

Making Sense of Exponents | © ironboxeducation.com | Log in for demo videos. 35

Key Points from Demo Video – Lesson 25

Factoring Quadratic Expressions

In Lesson 25, students practice factoring quadratic expressions (involving squares, or a base raised to the second power).

In Part 1, students factor the numbers 24, 30, and 36 (the same numbers as the diamond puzzles in the previous lesson).

Part 2 has two rows.

- In the first row, students factor quadratic expressions. There are no diamond puzzles to help them, but if necessary, they can draw a big "X" to work out the problem, as shown in Box D1. The constant (value without a variable) goes on the top of the diamond.
- In the second row, students multiply the factors to check their work. This involves multiplying binomials, just like in Lesson 9. The product should match the expression in the problem above.

The directions for Part 3 are the same as in Part 2.

KEY LESSON

Name____________________

Lesson 26: Factoring Quadratic Expressions to Simplify Fractions

Part 1: Follow along with your instructor to complete this lesson. Factor, then simplify.

A.	B.
$\frac{x^2 + 8x + 12}{x^2 + 14x + 48} = \frac{(x+6)(x+2)}{(x+6)(x+8)}$ $= \frac{x+2}{x+8}$	$\frac{n^2 + 9n + 20}{n^2 + 10n + 25} = \frac{(n+4)(n+5)}{(n+5)(n+5)}$ $= \frac{n+4}{n+5}$
C. $\frac{a^2 + 12a + 36}{a^2 + 8a + 12} = \frac{(a+6)(a+6)}{(a+6)(a+2)}$ $= \frac{a+6}{a+2}$	D. $\frac{m^2 + 17m + 72}{m + 4 + 4} = \frac{(m+8)(m+9)}{(m+8)}$ $= m + 9$

Part 2: Factor, simplify, then multiply.

E.
$\frac{n^2 + 10n + 21}{n^2 + 9n + 20} \cdot \frac{n^2 + 6n + 8}{n^2 + 5n + 6} = \frac{(n+3)(n+7)}{(n+4)(n+5)} \cdot \frac{(n+4)(n+2)}{(n+3)(n+2)}$

$= \frac{n+7}{n+5}$

F.
$\frac{y^2 + 8y + 15}{y^2 + 7y + 12} \cdot \frac{y^2 + 6y + 8}{y^2 + 7y + 10} = \frac{(y+5)(y+3)}{(y+3)(y+4)} \cdot \frac{(y+4)(y+2)}{(y+5)(y+2)}$

$= 1$

36 Making Sense of Exponents | © ironboxeducation.com | Log in for demo videos.

Key Points from Demo Video – Lesson 26

Factoring Quadratic Expressions to Simplify Fractions

As shown in the demo video, Lesson 26 is a prime example of how fluency in working with exponents helps students crack the code to higher level math.

In this lesson, students divide and multiply fractions that have quadratic expressions in both the numerator and denominator. Quadratic expressions involve squares (a base raised to the second power).

These problems look extremely difficult, but they are rather easy once students realize that they already have all the skills they need to solve them.

In Box A, students start by factoring each of the quadratic expressions. Factor one quadratic expression at a time, using an index card if necessary to cover up the visual clutter.

Once the quadratic expressions are factored, students will notice that they have a fraction that they can simplify since (x + 6) in the numerator cancels out (x + 6) in the denominator. Box A simplifies to (x + 2)/(x + 8), as shown in the answer key. The rest of the problems follow this same format.

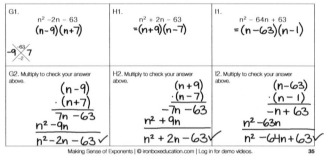

KEY LESSON Name________________

Lesson 27: Using the Distributive Property to Multiply Polynomials

Part 1: Follow along with your instructor to complete this lesson.

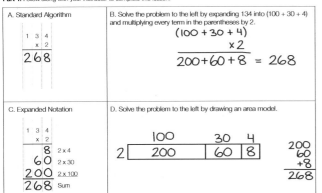

A. Standard Algorithm 134 x 2 268	B. Solve the problem to the left by expanding 134 into (100 + 30 + 4) and multiplying every term in the parentheses by 2. (100 + 30 + 4) x 2 200+60+8 = 268
C. Expanded Notation 134 x 2 8 2 x 4 60 2 x 30 200 2 x 100 268 Sum	D. Solve the problem to the left by drawing an area model. 100 30 4 2 | 200 | 60 | 8 | 200 60 +8 268

Part 2: Use the distributive property to multiply.

E.	F.	G.
$(s^2 + 5s + 6)$ x2 $2s^2+10s+12$	$(t^2 + 7t + 10)$ x7 $7t^2+49t+70$	$(u^2 + 5u + 6)$ x5u $5u^3+25u^2+30u$

Part 3: Use the distributive property to multiply. Multiply horizontally, and do not rewrite the problems vertically.

Example:	H.	I.
2(100 + 30 + 4) = 200+60+8 = 268	3(200 + 40 + 3) = 600+120+9 = 729	$2(s^2 + 5s + 6)$ $=2s^2+10s+12$
J.	**K.**	**L.**
$7(t^2 + 7t + 10)$ $=7t^2+49t+70$	$5u(u^2 + 5u + 6)$ $=5u^3+25u^2+30u$	$x^2(x^2 + x + 1)$ $=x^4+x^3+x^2$

Making Sense of Exponents | © ironboxeducation.com | Log in for demo videos. 37

Key Points from Demo Video – Lesson 27

Using the Distributive Property to Multiply Polynomials

Lesson 27 is similar to (and simpler than) Lesson 9 on multiplying binomials.

In this lesson, students will use the distributive property to learn the strong connection between the following:

- multiplying a three-digit number by a single-digit number
- multiplying a three-term polynomial (trinomial) by a single term

The demo video shows that in Part 1, students solve the problem 134 x 2 in four different ways. In Box A, students use the standard algorithm.

In Box B, students solve the same problem using an expanded approach. The number 134 is expanded into (100 + 30 + 4). Then, each term in the parentheses is multiplied by 2. This shows the distributive property.

In Parts 2 and 3, the distributive property is used to multiply a trinomial by a single term. Problems are solved both vertically and horizontally.

KEY LESSON Name________________

Lesson 28: Multiplying Binomials Using the FOIL Method

Part 1: In Lessons 9 and 10, you easily multiplied binomials using vertical multiplication. Complete the problems below.

A.	B.	B.
31 x 32 62 +930 992	(30 + 1) x(30 + 2) 60+2 900+30 900+90+2 =992	(n + 5) x(n + 6) 6n +30 n^2+5n $n^2+11n+30$

Part 2: You can also multiply binomials using the FOIL method. FOIL stands for **F**irst, **O**uter, **I**nner, and **L**ast. Complete the analogies below with your instructor.

A. Each tandem bicycle below has a rider who is first and a rider who is last. Label each rider on each tandem bicycle as ***"first"*** or ***"last."***

first last first last

B. Each set of parentheses below has a term that is first and a term that is last. Label each term in each set of parentheses as as ***"first"*** or ***"last."***

first last first last

(n + 5) (n + 6)

C. Look at the four bicyclists all in a row. Two of them have the inner position, and two have the outer position. Label the riders ***"inner"*** or ***"outer."***

outer inner inner outer

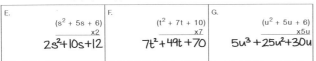

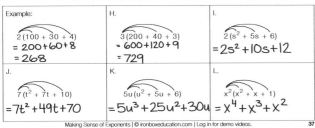

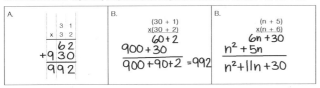

D. Look at the four terms all in a row. Two of them have the inner position, and two have the outer position. Label the terms ***"inner"*** or ***"outer."***

outer inner inner outer

(n + 5) (n + 6)

Part 3: To use the FOIL method, multiply the **F**irst terms, the **O**uter terms, the **I**nner terms, and the **L**ast terms. Multiply (n + 5)(n + 6). Then, simplify your answer by combining terms with the same bases (think "apples plus apples").

O F **(n + 5)(n + 6)** I L

E.

(n + 5)(n + 6)

$=n^2+(6n+5n)+30$

$=n^2+11n+30$

38 Making Sense of Exponents | © ironboxeducation.com | Log in for demo videos.

Key Points from Demo Video – Lesson 28

Multiplying Binomials Using the FOIL Method

In Lessons 9 and 10, students multiplied binomials using vertical multiplication. Now, students will multiply binomials using the FOIL method.

Part 1 provides a review of Lessons 9 and 10. Also, it reminds students that multiplying a binomial by a binomial is just like multiplying a two-digit number by a two-digit number.

Part 2 introduces the FOIL method. FOIL stands for First, Outer, Inner, and Last. With their instructor, students complete the analogies so that they understand what First, Outer, Inner, and Last mean when multiplying binomials.

The analogy uses two sets of tandem bicycles (with two riders each) to represent two sets of binomials (with two terms each).

Part 3 shows students how to use the FOIL method to multiply two binomials horizontally (instead of vertically). Multiply the First terms, the Outer terms, the Inner terms, and the Last terms, as shown in the diagram. Finally, simplify the product by combining terms with the same bases (think "apples plus apples").

KEY LESSON

Name____________________________

Lesson 29: Multiplying Binomials Using the FOIL Method (or the FIOL Method)

Directions: Multiply by using the FOIL method instead of using vertical multiplication. In each set of parentheses, multiply the **F**irst terms, the **I**nner terms, the **O**uter terms, and the **L**ast terms.

(a + 6)(a + 8) (F, O, I, L)

Important Note: *Visually, many students find it easier to go in this order instead: First, Inner, Outer, Last.* The reason for this is that after you multiply the *First* terms, your eyes are already looking at the Inner terms (which are also close together), so it's more convenient to multiply the Inner terms next. Then, multiply the Outer terms and the Last terms.

(a + 6)(a + 8) (F, I, L, O)

A. Try this order: First, Inner, Outer, Last. (a + 6)(a + 8) $=a^2+6a+8a+48$ $=a^2+14a+48$	B. (b + 6)(b + 9) $=b^2+6b+9b+54$ $=b^2+15b+54$	C. (c + 7)(c + 9) $=c^2+7c+9c+63$ $=c^2+16c+63$
D. (d + 6)(d + 6) $=d^2+6d+6d+36$ $=d^2+12d+36$	E. (e + 6)(e + 7) $=e^2+6e+7e+42$ $=e^2+13e+42$	F. (f + 6)(f + 5) $=f^2+6f+5f+30$ $=f^2+11f+30$
G. $(g+7)^2$ $=(g+7)(g+7)$ $=g^2+7g+7g+49$ $=g^2+14g+49$	H. $(h+8)^2$ $=(h+8)(h+8)$ $=h^2+8h+8h+64$ $=h^2+16h+64$	I. $(j+9)^2$ $=(j+9)(j+9)$ $=j^2+9j+9j+81$ $=j^2+18j+81$
J. (3k + 2)(k + 4) $=3k^2+2k+12k+8$ $=3k^2+14k+8$	K. (2m + 3)(m + 5) $=2m^2+3m+10m+15$ $=2m^2+13m+15$	L. (4n + 7)(n + 3) $=4n^2+7n+12n+21$ $=4n^2+19n+21$

Making Sense of Exponents | © ironboxeducation.com | Log in for demo videos. 39

Key Points from Demo Video – Lesson 29

Multiplying Binomials Using the FOIL Method (or the FIOL Method)

In Lesson 29, students practice using the FOIL method to multiply binomials horizontally. In Lessons 9 and 10, they multiplied binomials vertically.

An ***important note*** for this lesson is that visually, many students find it easier to go in this order instead: First, Inner, Outer, Last (FIOL).

The reason for this that after multiplying the *First* terms, students' eyes are already looking at the *Inner* terms (which are also close together), so it's more convenient to multiply the Inner terms next.

Then, multiply the Outer terms and the Last terms.

Whether students use FOIL or FIOL, the product will be the same, so students can use whatever method they find more comfortable.

KEY LESSON

Name____________________________

Lesson 30: Multiplying Binomials Using the FOIL Method (or the FIOL Method)

Part 1: Follow along with your instructor to complete this lesson. Add, subtract, or multiply.

A.	B.	C.	D.
3 + 5 = 8	5 + 3 = 8	3 · 5 = 15	5 · 3 = 15
3 + −5 = −2	5 + −3 = 2	3 · −5 = −15	5 · −3 = −15
−3 + 5 = 2	−5 + 3 = −2	−3 · 5 = −15	−5 · 3 = −15
−3 + −5 = −8	−5 + −3 = −8	−3 · −5 = 15	−5 · −3 = 15

Part 2: Multiply using the FOIL method. *Visually, many find it easier to go in this order instead: First, Inner, Outer, Last. The reason for this is that after you multiply the First terms, your eyes are already looking at the Inner terms (which are also close together), so it's more convenient to multiply the Inner terms next. Then, multiply the Outer terms and the Last terms.*

E. (x + 3)(x + 5) $=x^2+3x+5x+15$ $=x^2+8x+15$	F. (x + 3)(x − 5) $=x^2+3x-5x-15$ $=x^2-2x-15$	G. (x −3)(x + 5) $=x^2-3x+5x-15$ $=x^2+2x-15$
H. (x − 3)(x − 5) $=x^2-3x-5x+15$ $=x^2-8x+15$	I. (x − 5)(x − 3) $=x^2-5x-3x+15$ $=x^2-8x+15$	J. (x + 5)(x + 3) $=x^2+5x+3x+15$ $=x^2+8x+15$
K. (x + 5)(x − 3) $=x^2+5x-3x-15$ $=x^2+2x-15$	L. (x − 5)(x + 3) $=x^2-5x+3x-15$ $=x^2-2x-15$	M. (x − 3)(x − 5) $=x^2-3x-5x+15$ $=x^2-8x+15$

40 Making Sense of Exponents | © ironboxeducation.com | Log in for demo videos.

Key Points from Demo Video – Lesson 30

Multiplying Binomials Using the FOIL Method (or the FIOL Method)

In the previous two lessons, students multiplied binomials horizontally using the FOIL method (or the FIOL method).

In Lesson 30, students continue multiplying binomials, except these problems involve both positive and negative integers.

In Part 1, students review adding, subtracting, and multiplying integers, which they learned in the book *Making Sense of Integers*.

In Part 2, students multiply binomials. These problems are specially set up to have students focus closely on positive and negative signs when multiplying, adding, and subtracting terms.

As shown in the demo video, teach students to ***proceed deliberately*** with these problems, moving in a careful and unhurried way. Overlooking even a single integer will throw off the entire problem and cause confusion.

Remind students that fluency is not just about speed. It's also about smoothness and ease.

Name______________________________

Lesson 31: Multiplying Binomials Using the FOIL Method (or the FIOL Method)

Part 1: Add, subtract, or multiply.

A.	B.	C.	D.
$4 + 9 = 13$	$9 + 4 = 13$	$4 \cdot 9 = 36$	$9 \cdot 4 = 36$
$4 + {-9} = -5$	$9 + {-4} = 5$	$4 \cdot -9 = -36$	$9 \cdot -4 = -36$
$-4 + 9 = 5$	$-9 + 4 = -5$	$-4 \cdot 9 = -36$	$-9 \cdot 4 = -36$
$-4 + {-9} = -13$	$-9 + {-4} = -13$	$-4 \cdot -9 = 36$	$-9 \cdot -4 = 36$

Part 2: Multiply using the FOIL method. *Visually, many find it easier to go in this order instead: **F**irst, **I**nner, **O**uter, **L**ast. The reason for this is that after you multiply the First terms, your eyes are already looking at the Inner terms (which are also close together), so it's more convenient to multiply the Inner terms next. Then, multiply the Outer terms and the Last terms.*

E. $(x + 4)(x + 9)$ $= x^2 + 4x + 9x + 36$ $= x^2 + 13x + 36$	F. $(x + 4)(x - 9)$ $= x^2 + 4x - 9x - 36$ $= x^2 - 5x - 36$	G. $(x - 4)(x + 9)$ $= x^2 - 4x + 9x - 36$ $= x^2 + 5x - 36$
H. $(x - 4)(x - 9)$ $= x^2 - 4x - 9x + 36$ $= x^2 - 13x + 36$	I. $(x - 9)(x - 4)$ $= x^2 - 9x - 4x + 36$ $= x^2 - 13x + 36$	J. $(x + 9)(x + 4)$ $= x^2 + 9x + 4x + 36$ $= x^2 + 13x + 36$
K. $(x + 9)(x - 4)$ $= x^2 + 9x - 4x - 36$ $= x^2 + 5x - 36$	L. $(x - 9)(x + 4)$ $= x^2 - 9x + 4x - 36$ $= x^2 - 5x - 36$	M. $(x - 4)(x - 9)$ $= x^2 - 4x - 9x + 36$ $= x^2 - 13x + 36$

Making Sense of Exponents | © ironboxeducation.com | Log in for demo videos. 41

Key Points from Demo Video – Lesson 31

Multiplying Binomials Using the FOIL Method (or the FIOL Method)

In Lessons 29 and 30, students multiplied binomials horizontally using the FOIL method (or the FIOL method).

In Lesson 31, as in the previous lesson, students continue multiplying binomials, except these problems involve both positive and negative integers.

In Part 1, students review adding, subtracting, and multiplying integers, which they learned in the book *Making Sense of Integers*.

In Part 2, students multiply binomials. These problems are specially set up to have students focus closely on positive and negative signs when multiplying, adding, and subtracting terms.

As shown in the demo video, teach students to ***proceed deliberately*** with these problems, moving in a careful and unhurried way. Overlooking even a single integer will throw off the entire problem and cause confusion.

Remind students that fluency is not just about speed. It's also about smoothness and ease.

KEY LESSON

Name______________________________

Lesson 32: Adding and Subtracting Numbers with Exponents

In previous lessons you learned the following:

- You can only add and subtract ***objects*** if they have the <u>same name</u> (for example, "apples plus apples").
- You can only add and subtract ***fractions*** if they have the <u>same name</u> (denominator).
- You can only add and subtract ***variables with exponents*** if they have the <u>same name</u> (base and exponent).

This same concept applies to ***numbers with exponents*** as well. If numbers do not have the same base and exponent, you'll need to evaluate them first before adding and subtracting them.

Part 1: Follow along with your instructor to complete this lesson.

A.	B.	C.	D.
1 pencil +1 pencil 2 pencils	1 plant +1 radio 1 plant + 1 radio	1 third +1 third 2 thirds	1 half +1 third 1 half + 1 third
E.	**F.**	**G.**	**H.**
$5x^2y$ $+3x^2y$ $8x^2y$	$5x^2y^2$ $+3x^2y$ $5x^2y^2 + 3x^2y$	3 thousand +4 thousand 7 thousand	3 million +4 thousand 3 million + 4 thousand

Part 2: Simplify. Leave all your answers in exponential form. Remember that ***variables with exponents*** and ***numbers with exponents*** can only be added and subtracted if they have the same base and exponent.

I1. $a^4 + (a^{-5} + a^{-5})$ $= a^4 + 2a^{-5}$	J1. $b^4 + b^4 + b^4$ $= 3b^4$	K1. $c^{10} + (c^9 + c^9 + c^9)$ $= c^{10} + 3c^9$	L1. $(d^3 + d^3 + d^3) + d^{-4}$ $= 3d^3 + d^{-4}$
I2. $7^4 + (7^{-5} + 7^{-5})$ $= 7^4 + 2(7^{-5})$	J2. $11^4 + 11^4 + 11^4$ $= 3(11^4)$	K2. $8^{10} + (8^9 + 8^9 + 8^9)$ $= 8^{10} + 3(8^9)$	L2. $(9^3 + 9^3 + 9^3) + 9^{-4}$ $= 3(9^3) + 9^{-4}$
M. $(10^6 + 10^6) + (10^3 + 10^3 + 10^3 + 10^3) + 10^2$ $= 2(10^6) + 4(10^3) + 10^2$		N. $10^6 + 10^3 + (10^2 + 10^2 + 10^2 + 10^2) + 10^0$ $= 10^6 + 10^3 + 4(10^2) + 10^0$	

42 Making Sense of Exponents | © ironboxeducation.com | Log in for demo videos.

Key Points from Demo Video – Lesson 32

Adding and Subtracting Numbers with Exponents

Previously, students learned to add and subtract ***variables with exponents*** such as $b^4 + b^4$.

In this lesson, students will add and subtract ***numbers with exponents*** such as $11^4 + 11^4$.

Students already know the following:

- You can only add and subtract ***objects*** if they have the <u>same name</u> (for example, "apples plus apples").
- You can only add and subtract ***fractions*** if they have the <u>same name</u> (denominators).
- You can only add and subtract ***variables with exponents*** if they have the <u>same name</u> (base and exponent).

Following this same logic, you can only add and subtract ***numbers with exponents*** if they have the <u>same name</u> (base and exponent).

As shown in the demo video, this lesson helps build this intuition. It does so by using analogies between variables with exponents (Part 2, Row 1), and numbers with exponents (Part 2, Row 2).

KEY LESSON

Name____________________

Lesson 33: Adding, Subtracting, and Multiplying Numbers with Exponents

Part 1: Simplify. Leave your answers in exponential form.

A. Expand first, then simplify. $17^3 \cdot 17^3$ $=17\cdot17\cdot17\cdot17\cdot17\cdot17$ $=17^6$	B. Simplify without expanding. $17^9 \cdot 17^{-4}$ $=17^5$	C. Write as a fraction. $17^9 \cdot 17^{-11}$ $=17^{-2}$ $=\frac{1}{17^2}$	D. Write as a fraction. $23^4 \cdot 17^{-9}$ $=\frac{23^4}{17^9}$

Part 2: Simplify. Leave your answers in exponential form. Remember that ***variables with exponents*** and ***numbers with exponents*** can only be added and subtracted if they have the same base and exponent.

E. $17^4+(17^3+17^3)$ $=17^4+2(17^3)$	F. $17^9+(17^4+17^4+17^4)$ $=17^9+3(17^4)$	G. $17^9+17^9+17^9+17^9$ $=4(17^9)$	H. $(17^9+17^9+17^9)+17^4$ $=3(17^9)+17^4$

Part 3: Evaluate. Remember that a number raised to the zero power equals 1.

I. $(2^{13}\cdot2^{-10})+2^4$ $=2^3+2^4$ $=8+16$ $=24$	J. $2^3+(2^{-3}\cdot2^5)$ $=2^3+2^2$ $=8+4$ $=12$	K. $(3^{25}\cdot3^{-22})+3^2$ $=3^3+3^2$ $=27+9$ $=36$	L. 3^0+3^{-2} $=1+\frac{1}{3^2}$ $=1+\frac{1}{9}$ $=1\frac{1}{9}$

Part 4: Evaluate. Remember that a number raised to the zero power equals 1.

M.

$10^0 =$ 1	$10^3 =$ 1,000	$10^6 =$ 1,000,000
$10^1 =$ 10	$10^4 =$ 10,000	$10^7 =$ 10,000,000
$10^2 =$ 100	$10^5 =$ 100,000	$10^8 =$ 100,000,000

Part 5: Evaluate. Remember that a number raised to the zero power equals 1.

N. $(10^6+10^6)+(10^3+10^3+10^3+10^3)+10^0$ $=2(10^6)+4(10^3)+10^0$ $=2(1{,}000{,}000)+4(1{,}000)+1$ $=2{,}004{,}001$	O. $10^6+10^3+(10^2+10^2+10^2+10^2)$ $=10^6+10^3+4(10^2)$ $=1{,}000{,}000+1{,}000+4(100)$ $=1{,}001{,}400$

Making Sense of Exponents | © ironboxeducation.com | Log in for demo videos. 43

Key Points from Demo Video – Lesson 33

Adding, Subtracting, and Multiplying with Exponents

Lesson 33 builds upon the previous lesson, which involved ***adding and subtracting*** numbers with exponents.

Additionally, this lesson includes ***multiplying*** numbers with exponents. This will help students notice the the differences between adding and subtracting numbers with exponents versus multiplying numbers with exponents.

Part 3 involves both multiplying numbers with exponents as adding numbers with exponents. Students must evaluate each expression, as shown in the answer key. Box I, J, and K will be whole numbers, and Box L will be a mixed number (a whole number and a fraction).

Part 4 and Part 5 go together. In Part 4, students review powers of 10. In Part 5, students evaluate expressions that involve powers of ten. Keep the following in mind:

- $10^6 = 1{,}000{,}000$ (one million)
- $10^3 = 1{,}000$ (one thousand)
- $10^0 = 1$ (one)

KEY LESSON

Name____________________

Lesson 34: Comparing Numbers with Exponents

Part 1: Expand, then evaluate. Notice the patterns that result in each row.

A. $(-2)^2$ $=(-2)(-2)$ $=4$	B. $(-2)^3$ $=(-2)(-2)(-2)$ $=-8$	C. $(-2)^4$ $=(-2)(-2)(-2)(-2)$ $=16$	D. $(-2)^5$ $=(-2)(-2)(-2)(-2)(-2)$ $=-32$
E. $-(2^2)$ $=-(2\cdot2)$ $=-4$	F. $-(2^3)$ $=-(2\cdot2\cdot2)$ $=-8$	G. $-(2^4)$ $=-(2\cdot2\cdot2\cdot2)$ $=-16$	H. $-(2^5)$ $=-(2\cdot2\cdot2\cdot2\cdot2)$ $=-32$
I. $(-2)^{-2}$ $=\frac{1}{(-2)(-2)}$ $=\frac{1}{4}$	J. $(-2)^{-3}$ $=\frac{1}{(-2)(-2)(-2)}$ $=-\frac{1}{8}$	K. $(-2)^{-4}$ $=\frac{1}{(-2)(-2)(-2)(-2)}$ $=\frac{1}{16}$	L. $(-2)^{-5}$ $=\frac{1}{(-2)(-2)(-2)(-2)(-2)}$ $=-\frac{1}{32}$
M. $-(2^{-2})$ $=-\frac{1}{2\cdot2}$ $=-\frac{1}{4}$	N. $-(2^{-3})$ $=-\frac{1}{2\cdot2\cdot2}$ $=-\frac{1}{8}$	O. $-(2^{-4})$ $=-\frac{1}{2\cdot2\cdot2\cdot2}$ $=-\frac{1}{16}$	P. $-(2^{-5})$ $=-\frac{1}{2\cdot2\cdot2\cdot2\cdot2}$ $=-\frac{1}{32}$

Pattern in Row 1 (Boxes A-D): alternating positive and negative

Pattern in Row 2 (Boxes E-H): all negative

Pattern in Row 3 (Boxes I-L): alternating positive and negative fractions

Pattern in Row 4 (Boxes M-P): all negative fractions

Part 2: Use the symbols greater than (>), less than (<), or equal to (=) to compare exponents. Show your work.

Q. $(-2)^2 > -(2^2)$ $4 > -4$	R. $(-2)^3 = -(2^3)$ $-8 = -8$	S. $-(2^4) < (-2)^4$ $-16 < 16$
T. $-(2^2) < -(2^{-2})$ $-4 < -\frac{1}{4}$	U. $(-2)^4 > (-2)^{-4}$ $16 > \frac{1}{16}$	V. $(-2)^5 < -(2^{-5})$ $-32 < -\frac{1}{32}$

44 Making Sense of Exponents | © ironboxeducation.com | Log in for demo videos.

Key Points from Demo Video – Lesson 34

Comparing Numbers with Exponents

In Part 1, students expand then evaluate each expression. Students should notice the patterns that result in each row.

- Row 1: alternating positive and negative
- Row 2: all negative
- Row 3: alternating positive and negative fractions
- Row 4: all negative fractions

Also, Part 1 helps students notice that subtle differences in grouping result in different values. For example, $(-2)^2 = 4$, but $-2^2 = -4$.

The order of operations (P E MD AS) helps explain this. In Box A, the expression $(-2)^2$ means $(-2)(-2)$, which equals 4. The base of (-2) is squared.

In Box E, the expression -2^2 means $-(2^2)$, which equals -4. In the order of operations, since exponents come before multiplication, the base of 2 must be squared first, then multiplied by -1.

In Part 2, students use the symbols greater than (>), less than (<), or equal to (=) to compare numbers with exponents. Use the empty white space in each box to evaluate each expression before comparing.

Name________________________________

Lesson 35: Comparing Numbers with Exponents

Part 1: Expand, then evaluate. Notice the patterns that result in each row.

A. $-(10^2)$ $=-(10\cdot10)$ $=-100$	B. $-(10^3)$ $=-(10\cdot10\cdot10)$ $=-1{,}000$	C. $-(10^4)$ $=-(10\cdot10\cdot10\cdot10)$ $=-10{,}000$	D. $-(10^5)$ $=-(10\cdot10\cdot10\cdot10\cdot10)$ $=-100{,}000$
E. $(-10)^2$ $=(-10)(-10)$ $=100$	F. $(-10)^3$ $=(-10)(-10)(-10)$ $=-1{,}000$	G. $(-10)^4$ $=(-10)(-10)(-10)(-10)$ $=10{,}000$	H. $(-10)^5$ $=(-10)(-10)(-10)(-10)(-10)$ $=-100{,}000$
I. $-(10^{-2})$ $=-\frac{1}{10\cdot10}$ $=-\frac{1}{100}$	J. $-(10^{-3})$ $=-\frac{1}{10\cdot10\cdot10}$ $=-\frac{1}{1{,}000}$	K. $-(10^{-4})$ $=-\frac{1}{10\cdot10\cdot10\cdot10}$ $=-\frac{1}{10{,}000}$	L. $-(10^{-5})$ $=-\frac{1}{10\cdot10\cdot10\cdot10\cdot10}$ $=-\frac{1}{100{,}000}$
M. $(-10)^{-2}$ $=\frac{1}{(-10)(-10)}$ $=\frac{1}{100}$	N. $(-10)^{-3}$ $=\frac{1}{(-10)(-10)(-10)}$ $=-\frac{1}{1{,}000}$	O. $(-10)^{-4}$ $=\frac{1}{(-10)(-10)(-10)(-10)}$ $=\frac{1}{10{,}000}$	P. $(-10)^{-5}$ $=\frac{1}{(-10)(-10)(-10)(-10)(-10)}$ $=-\frac{1}{100{,}000}$

Pattern in Row 1 (Boxes A-D): all negative

Pattern in Row 2 (Boxes E-H): alternating positive and negative

Pattern in Row 3 (Boxes I-L): all negative fractions

Pattern in Row 4 (Boxes M-P): alternating positive and negative fractions

Part 2: Use the symbols greater than (>), less than (<), or equal to (=) to compare exponents. Show your work.

Q. $-(10^2) < -(10^{-2})$ $-100 < -\frac{1}{100}$	R. $(-10)^5 < -(10^{-5})$ $-100{,}000 < -\frac{1}{100{,}000}$	S. $(-10)^4 > (-10)^{-4}$ $10{,}000 > \frac{1}{10{,}000}$
T. $(-10)^3 = -(10^3)$ $-1{,}000 = -1{,}000$	U. $(-10)^2 > -(10^2)$ $100 > -100$	V. $-(10^4) < (-10)^4$ $-10{,}000 < 10{,}000$

Making Sense of Exponents | © ironboxeducation.com | Log in for demo videos. 45

Key Points from Demo Video – Lesson 35

Comparing Numbers with Exponents

In Part 1, students expand then evaluate each expression. Students should notice the patterns that result in each row.

- Row 1: all negative
- Row 2: alternating positive and negative
- Row 3: all negative fractions
- Row 4: alternating positive and negative fractions

Also, Part 1 helps students notice that subtle differences in grouping result in different values. For example, $-10^2 = -100$, but $(-10)^2 = 100$.

The order of operations (P E MD AS) helps explain this. In Box A, the expression -10^2 means $-(10^2)$, which equals -100. In the order of operations, since exponents come before multiplication, the base of 10 must be squared first, then multiplied by -1.

In Box E, the expression $(-10)^2$ means $(-10)(-10)$, which equals 100. The base of (-10) is squared.

In Part 2, students use the symbols greater than (>), less than (<), or equal to (=) to compare numbers with exponents. Use the empty white space in each box to evaluate each expression before comparing.

KEY LESSON

Name________________________________

Lesson 36: Comparing Fractions with Exponents

Part 1: Follow along with your instructor. Expand, then evaluate. Notice the patterns from row to row.

- Row 1: **The number 1** is raised to second, third, and fourth powers.
- Row 2: **A number greater than 1** is raised to second, third, and fourth powers.
- Row 3: **A fraction** is raised to second, third, and fourth powers.
- Row 4: **The number 0** is raised to second, third, and fourth powers.

A. $1^2 = 1\cdot1$ $=1$	B. $1^3 = 1\cdot1\cdot1$ $=1$	C. $1^4 = 1\cdot1\cdot1\cdot1$ $=1$
D. $2^2 = 2\cdot2$ $=4$	E. $2^3 = 2\cdot2\cdot2$ $=8$	F. $2^4 = 2\cdot2\cdot2\cdot2$ $=16$
G. $(\frac{1}{2})^2 = \frac{1}{2}\cdot\frac{1}{2} = \frac{1}{4}$ 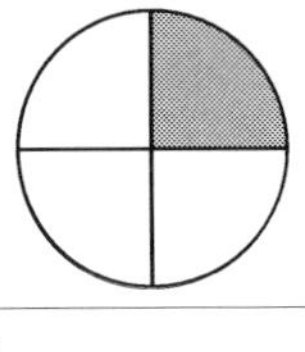	H. $(\frac{1}{2})^3 = \frac{1}{2}\cdot\frac{1}{2}\cdot\frac{1}{2} = \frac{1}{8}$ 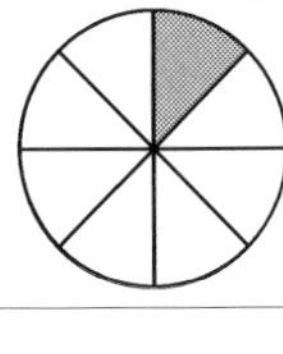	I. $(\frac{1}{2})^4 = \frac{1}{2}\cdot\frac{1}{2}\cdot\frac{1}{2}\cdot\frac{1}{2} = \frac{1}{16}$ 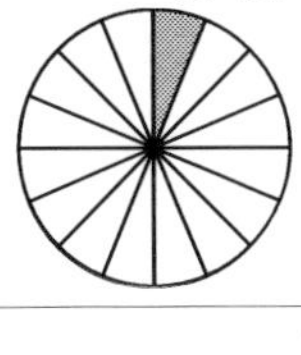
J. $0^2 = 0\cdot0$ $=0$	K. $0^3 = 0\cdot0\cdot0$ $=0$	L. $0^4 = 0\cdot0\cdot0\cdot0$ $=0$

Part 2: Use the symbols greater than (>), less than (<), or equal to (=) to compare by inspection.

M. $(\frac{1}{8})^3 < (\frac{1}{8})^2$	N. $(\frac{2}{3})^5 < (\frac{2}{3})^2$	O. $(\frac{3}{5})^5 > (\frac{3}{5})^9$
P. $(\frac{7}{9})^6 > (\frac{7}{9})^8$	Q. Hint: Simplify the fraction first. $(\frac{6}{3})^2 < (\frac{6}{3})^3$ $2^2 < 2^3$	R. Hint: Convert to a mixed number first. $(\frac{3}{2})^2 < (\frac{3}{2})^3$ $(1\frac{1}{2})^2 < (1\frac{1}{2})^3$

46 Making Sense of Exponents | © ironboxeducation.com | Log in for demo videos.

Key Points from Demo Video – Lesson 36

Comparing Fractions with Exponents

In Lesson 36, students follow along with their instructor to compare fractions with exponents.

In Part 1, students expand and evaluate each expression. They should notice the patterns from row to row, as explained in the directions.

Row 3 (Boxes G, H, and I) shows that as a fraction is raised to higher powers, the values get progressively smaller. This is also shown by shading in the fraction circle.

In Part 2, students use the symbols greater than (>), less than (<), or equal to (=) to compare fractions with exponents.

These problems should be solved by inspection and not by actually working out the problems. As shown in the demo video, use your observations from Part 1 as a shortcut to see the answers at a glance.

In Box Q, simplify the fractions first, which will give you a whole number greater than 1.

In Box R, convert the fractions to mixed numbers first, which will give you a value greater than 1.

84206819R00038

Made in the USA
San Bernardino, CA
06 August 2018